Students Are Stakeholders, Too!

Students Are Stakeholders, Too!

Including Every Voice in Authentic High School Reform

EDIE L. HOLCOMB
Foreword by Shirley M. Hord

A Joint Publication

CORWIN PRESS
A SAGE Publications Company
Thousand Oaks, CA 91320

NATIONAL ASSOCIATION
OF SECONDARY SCHOOL
PRINCIPALS

For information:

Corwin Press
A Sage Publications Company
2455 Teller Road
Thousand Oaks, California 91320
www.corwinpress.com

Sage Publications Ltd.
1 Oliver's Yard
55 City Road
London EC1Y 1SP
United Kingdom

Sage Publications India Pvt. Ltd.
B-42, Panchsheel Enclave
Post Box 4109
New Delhi 110 017 India

Printed in the United States of America

Library of Congress Cataloging-in-Publication Data

Holcomb, Edie L.
Students are stakeholders, too!: Including every voice in authentic high school reform / Edie L. Holcomb.
 p. cm.
Includes bibliographical references and index.
ISBN 0-7619-2969-X or 978-0-7619-2969-7 (cloth)
ISBN 0-7619-2970-3 or 978-0-7619-2970-3 (pbk.)
 1. High schools—Administration. 2. Student participation in administration.
3. School environment. 4. School management and organization.
5. School improvement programs. I. Title.

LB2822.H64 2007
373.12—dc22

                                                    2006022365
This book is printed on acid-free paper.

06 07 08 09 10 9 8 7 6 5 4 3 2 1

Acquisitions Editor:	Robert D. Clouse
Editorial Assistant:	Jessica Wochna
Production Editor:	Denise Santoyo
Copy Editor:	Barbara Coster
Typesetter:	C&M Digitals (P) Ltd.
Indexer:	Jean Casalegno
Cover Designer:	Lisa Miller

Contents

List of Figures

Foreword

In all my years and experiences I have never encountered a book such as this one. It is, in a word, *superb*. No one has "covered the beat" of student roles in high school reform as Holcomb has. She brings the high school student body, as well as the teachers and the administrators, to life in all their richness and weirdness. We learn of these kids' angst, their courage, their brilliant ideas, and their commitment to making life and their learning better in their high school community. We learn how the principal began to open doors so that staff, challenged and catalyzed by the students, rallied to improve the conditions and practice of learning in their school.

Holcomb writes with candor and care, with persistence but patience, and with passion and concern about the individuals that inhabit Knownwell High School. We experience the anxiety of Norris; we celebrate the courage of Morris; and we become very good friends with all of the students who represent the broad spectrum of kids in this composite high school. The school, its staff, and the students represent the reality of all those individuals who live in every high school in America, or at least in those high schools that are making efforts to enhance the effectiveness of staff and increase student outcomes.

This work isn't just a story, albeit a very clever and meaningful one. The author gives us a set of eight "puzzles" that engage our attention and onto which we can hang the subsequent text. A set of four "premises" reveals Holcomb's beliefs and, consequently, values about the high school and its mission in our education system. With these introductory ideas and notions conveyed, the story begins.

But the story is interrupted at various critical junctures, and Questions for Reflection are provided. These questions invite the reader to reflect on the characters and their actions in the text in order to apply or relate them to the reader's own situation. These questions prompt the reader to stop and give attention and thought to the shared text of the school journey and how one can use it to inform one's own educational improvement strategies and activities.

In addition, references and material from the published literature are reported in a section on Content for Consideration. In these sections, sprinkled throughout the manuscript, Holcomb provides supporting information and commentary from other writers and projects focused on high school reform and on student roles and participation. These sections give the reader validation that supports the real possibility and effectiveness of the roles and activities in which students may contribute to their school's improvement goals.

Who should read this book? Anyone interested in or actively engaged in secondary school change and improvement is the target audience. This includes those who are internal to the school and those external, such as central office, external assistance providers, or intermediate service agencies, parents, community members. The book nicely balances the chronicle of change with accounts of the research and published literature from academics and scholars. This gives substance and validation to what might otherwise be a pie-in-the-sky narrative.

A most important person for reading this book and considering its possibilities for a school is the principal. It is the principal who, as Holcomb says and the research on the principalship confirms, is the gatekeeper to new ideas and the culture keeper for how things operate or work in a school. The principal's role is easily recognized and understood in Holcomb's book and reflects the reality of change in all schools.

A most important reason for the wide readership of this book is its promotion of the democratic participation of all the players in the school setting, centering on the students. Here, the leaders of today and tomorrow are developed: in creating new ideas for their schools, in learning the necessary skills for promoting ideas, and in honing interpersonal attributes or qualities that support the implementation of the ideas. For many, this premise is new, unknown, and uncomfortable. Holcomb's text has made, for me, the idea of students as stakeholders in the school a most understood and desirable phenomenon. It will do the same for other readers as well.

Shirley M. Hord, Scholar Emerita
Southwest Educational Development Laboratory
Austin, Texas

Preface

Students Are Stakeholders, Too! is the fifth book I've written on change in schools. The others were written with a focus on school leadership teams. As noted in Chapter 2, "Puzzles and Premises," I made reference in the previous books to students as stakeholders represented on the leadership team. But that's about as far as I got. I also referenced use of data, especially in the first and second editions of *Getting Excited About Data*. That almost got me pigeonholed into a reputation as a testing person. I'm not. I'm a passionate holder of high expectations for what can happen in schools when *all* members of the school community work together. And I've been desperately disappointed in the number of examples of where this actually occurs, especially in high schools. In my roles as a supervisor of schools and as a consultant, I have looked for examples that could be models. I wrote this book because I couldn't find them. I found books that included research about students. I found books that, like my own, recommended student involvement in decision making. I found books that summarized what students say when they are asked. I found books about schools that had changed for the better, but they seemed to talk about the roles of the principal only or the staff only. And they might tell about what changes had been made but not how they played out in real time. I couldn't find the book I wanted—so I have tried to write it.

WHAT THIS BOOK IS

It is the toughest writing I have ever done and took the longest. I didn't have a complete case study to document, because what I had seen were excellent pieces in a variety of places in the United States and Canada. I needed to create a composite, and it needed to flow naturally. It needed to be the story of a journey as it unfolded, and it needed to capture the dialogue and interaction that must occur. I tried to invent a neutral, fictitious setting in which to place all my notes and thoughts, and it was beyond my creativity. So I turned for the physical setting to a school I know well, where many of the things described have actually taken place and where all of them could. And I built around it. Every person in this story is modeled after a real person (or many) that I have seen in action. Everything that occurs at Knownwell High School has actually happened in at least one real-life school. I hope this book paints a picture of what can happen when a principal begins to seek and hear student voice and opens doors for greater interaction among adults and students.

WHAT THIS BOOK IS NOT

This book is not a composite of research about high school reform. Others have done that better than I. It's the story of a high school re-forming.

This book is not fiction, though it is semifictionalized in order to combine a range of settings and experiences. It may seem idealized, but everything that happens here has happened (even students coming forward to confess to misdeeds). If it sounds too perfect, read more closely and you will sense the resistance and barriers. I chose not to dwell upon them, because my purpose is to create a can-do picture, an alternative vision. And I chose not to paint resisters with a broad brush of criticism. The epilogues that close the book were co-written with some of the actual persons upon whom the book's characters are based. Their reflections reveal the real-world challenges that are inherent in change.

This book does not take issue with the value of small schools. (Students who reviewed the manuscript and wrote the epilogues with me were not prompted to discuss the size of their schools, and I was surprised when they did.) My purpose here is to paint a picture of how an ordinary school, with only its existing resources, can engage students and create a student-learning-centered culture. Schools I visited and combined here serve from 200 to 2,000, yet students had remarkably similar things to say.

This book is not written in a formal or technical style. It has been reviewed by several principals who attest to its reality and doability. And it has been reviewed by teenagers, who have helped me use their voice. Over the course of this work, youthful expressions have faded and been replaced with others, but as my granddaughter so diligently reminded me, "Things change faster than you could write the book anyway. But it doesn't sound phony or old." I'm immensely relieved.

This book may not appear to be multicultural, because I have tried and then discarded the use of ethnic names. Each character represents a subset of a student population—from Joe, the "big man on campus," to Mike, the skateboarder, to Teri, the special education student, to Gloria, the almost-gone-Goth. Whenever I tried to attach ethnic names to capture a diverse population, it seemed to stereotype whole groups into specific character types. I stuck with Morris as the name for our Everyman because I was so impressed by Ted Sizer's description of a school from the perspective of teacher Horace—and because I knew the name Morris as that of a hard-working Russian immigrant. Come to America and find your dream. Visit Knownwell High School and see a dream unfold.

HOW TO READ THIS BOOK

So that the book can serve many purposes, Questions for Reflection and Content for Consideration have been interspersed. As author, I would ask you to skip them at first and just read the story as it flows—starting in September of Year 3, to set the stage, and then flashing back to September of Year 1 and experiencing the two-year journey without interruption.

Read this book as an idealist and a visionary. Read it as a dreamer. Recall the line from the movie—"Build it and they will come."

Or read the book as a pragmatist. Look for the practical ways in which time was found and involvement was built.

Or go ahead and read it as a skeptic. Challenge yourself with the reflection questions. Study the Content for Consideration. If you find even 10% believable and feasible, act on the 10%. You will discover more if you take the first step.

Above all, read this book with awe and humility—not for my writing, but for the administrators, teachers, and students who have inspired it. Their actions have assured me that there is a foundation for my belief that students can help us shape better schools—and that, in doing so, they will learn lessons that will help them shape a better world.

Acknowledgments

Because this has been a different and difficult writing task, many acknowledgments are in order and I plead forgiveness from those who should be mentioned that I may miss. Every person who has heard about this project has urged me to continue and has provided me with reasons why it's needed or ideas to include. My heartfelt thanks extend even to the unknown seatmates on airplanes and tablemates at conferences who have encouraged me. I must especially acknowledge some "real school people," some special student voices, and the hands-on helpers who have made this possible.

REAL SCHOOL PEOPLE

- G. M. (Gordon) Bullivant, Executive Director, Foothills Academy, Calgary, Alberta—for hosting my visit and for introducing me to James, Sean, Alex, and Luke
- Steve Clarke, Principal, and the staff of Bellingham High School—for all that I learned from and with you, for supporting each other in good times and bad, and for donning academic regalia and turning out in force each year to show how much you value your graduates. I miss you.
- Bill Dickson, University of Calgary Adjunct Professor and Alberta Initiative for School Improvement Coordinator—for coordination of school visits in Calgary and hosting me at Calgary Alternative High School
- Becky Elmendorf, Principal, and the staff of Squalicum High School—for sharing what you would have done the same and different in your change efforts. Happy retirement, Becky!
- Manny Ferreirinha, Supervisor of Professional Development, Calgary Roman Catholic Separate School District No. 1—for hosting me in Edmonton and explaining Alberta education issues and funding for public and private schools
- A. John Fischer, Principal, Alternative High School, Calgary Board of Education—for supporting my visit, championing your students, and incorporating the values of First Nation culture

- Albert Herscovitch, Chartered Psychologist, Coordinator of the Rosscarrock Community and Family Support Program, Calgary Board of Education—for sharing about your Building Student Capacity in Resilience project and for hosting my visit to Foothills Academy
- Jim Kistner, Principal, and the staff of Sehome High School—for letting me see inside your peer coaching struggles and complimenting me with your candor. Don't fall off any more mountains, Jim!
- Ed Kupka and Susan Savaglio-Jarvis, Principal and Assistant Principal of Tremper High School—for embarking on a courageous journey of change and including me as a fellow "first-year" traveler
- Ginette Marshall, Alternative High School, Calgary Board of Education—for taking me on a tour of the school and introducing me to Amanda, Kurt, Gerald, Andrew, and Paul

SOME SPECIAL STUDENT VOICES

- Scott Frost—for student leadership, for taking risks to actively engage with the site planning team, and for finding time to add "one more thing" on short notice
- Gina Holcomb—for completion of one degree and charging after the next
- Kacie Holcomb—for graduation reflections on life in and out of high school, for love and loyalty, and for chasing the same dream
- Danielle (Nellie) Holcomb—for your unique blend of horsewoman and honor student that reminds me there is life outside of school too
- Melanie Hornung—for your perseverance and patience, and for adopting me
- Kelsey Swiatko—for your initiative and for answering the e-mails of an inquiring stranger

THE HANDS-ON HELPERS

- Judy Margrath-Huge—for being my friend, colleague, and provider of resources and insights about small schools and the work of the Bill and Melinda Gates Foundation
- Louise Mattioli—for handing me books and articles and also fussing over my pace and pulse
- Georgia Nisich—for staying after hours to answer my "how to" questions, for chasing references, for juggling my calendar, and for dealing patiently with occasional attacks of overload
- Dave Pedersen—for once again turning sketchy ideas into helpful figures

- And a special acknowledgment to Robb Clouse—for sticking with me as my Corwin editor, waiting for this project, and—I am *convinced*—conspiring with my husband to practice a perverted form of motivation. In the same week last fall, I got two messages, almost identical. "Realizing that with your current job and obligations and [. . . blah-blah-blah . . .] you can only do so much, and we might need to let you off the hook on this one." Well, gentlemen, thanks anyway—it's done!

—Edie Holcomb

Corwin Press gratefully acknowledges the contributions of the following people:

Karen Tichy, Associate Superintendent for Instruction
Catholic Education Office, St. Louis, MO

Donald Poplau, Principal
Mankato East High School, Mankato, MN

Gina Marx, Assistant Superintendent
Augusta Public Schools, Augusta, KS

Paul Young, Past President, NAESP
Executive Director, West After School Center, Lancaster, OH

Dan Lawson, Superintendent
Tullahoma City Schools, Tullahoma, TN

Rosemarie Young, Past President, NAESP
Principal, Watson Lane Elementary School, Louisville, KY

Erin A. Rivers, English Teacher, High School
Shawnee Mission School District, Overland Park, KS

Benjamin O. Canada, Associate Executive Director, District Services
Texas Association of School Boards, Round Rock, TX

About the Author

 **Edie L. Holcomb,** PhD, is Executive Director of Curriculum and Instructional Services, Kenosha Unified School District No. 1, in Kenosha, Wisconsin. She has experienced the challenges of improving student achievement from many perspectives:

- From classroom teacher to university professor
- From gifted-education coordinator to mainstream teacher of children with multiple disabilities
- From school- and district-level administration to national and international consulting
- From small rural districts to the challenges of urban education

She is highly regarded for her ability to link research and practice on issues related to instructional leadership and school and district change—including standards-based curriculum, instruction, assessment, supervision, and accountability. She has taught at all grade levels, served as a building principal and central office administrator, and assisted districts as an external facilitator for accreditation and implementation of school reform designs. As Associate Director of the National Center for Effective Schools, she developed a training program for site-based teams and provided technical support for implementation of school improvement efforts throughout the United States and in Canada, Guam, St. Lucia, and Hong Kong. She developed a comprehensive standards-based learning system for the staff and 47,000 students of the Seattle, Washington, city district and has supervised K–12 clusters of schools and evaluated principals.

Her work received the Excellence in Staff Development Award from the Iowa Association of Supervision and Curriculum Development in 1988. In 1990, her study of the needs of beginning principals was recognized by the American Association of School Administrators as recipient of the Paul F. Salmon Award for Outstanding Education Leadership Research.

She served as an elected member-at-large on the Leadership Council for ASCD International, played an active role in Washington State's School Improvement Assistance Program, and contributed to development of the new *School System Improvement Resource Guide*. She is scheduled to give presentations in Maine, Missouri, North Carolina, Ohio, Pennsylvania, Virginia, Washington State, Washington, DC, and Alberta and Saskatchewan in Canada.

She is the author of four previous books and numerous articles and reviews. Many schools and districts use the second editions of *Asking the Right Questions: Techniques for Collaboration and School Change* (2001) and *Getting Excited About Data: Combining People, Passion, and Proof to Maximize Student Achievement* (2004) as guidance for their improvement efforts. She can be reached at ELHolcomb@aol.com.

September, Year 3

Norris Starts at Knownwell High School

"**M**ah-ahm!" Norris stretched the maternal term into two syllables as he fidgeted on the car seat. "Would you stop worrying about me?! I'll be fine. I can't wait. Just let me out before someone sees us sitting here talking. It's just not cool."

"But, honey, what if you don't know anyone here? This isn't the high school that most of your middle school friends will be at this year."

"I know, Mom. They changed some boundaries around. But I still want to go here. We picked it, remember. Because people know each other here and care about each other. Sure, it didn't used to have the best reputation. But, you know, Mom, *Morris fixed all that!* Even though he graduated last year, everybody remembers how he got people to listen to what students were thinking."

"Well, I did hear a lot about your older brother at parent orientation, but it's hard to believe that a school could be changed by one kid asking questions and getting some other kids involved too. I guess I really didn't catch on to what Morris was talking about the last two years."

"Most of you adults just don't get it, do you? You think all we have going in our heads is rap music and sex. But that's OK, Mom. Don't sweat it, OK? You're not as bad as *some* grown-ups. Remember—I already know the principal and my adviser and my mentor, and I'll meet the other kids in my advisory today. Look, my mentor is standing there waiting for me right now. It's not like when I started *kindergarten*, you know."

"I know, son. I've met the principal and your adviser too. Have a good day . . . but, um, be sure you call me if you need anything."

"Yeah—right. Just relax, Mom. See you tonight." Turning his head to hide his involuntary adolescent eye-roll, Norris grabbed his backpack and stepped out onto the sidewalk. Then he remembered the extra effort his parents exerted to get his choice of school and the transportation they would be providing, and leaned back into the car to say, "Thanks for driving me, Mom. It won't be forever. I'll get friends to ride with, and I'll figure out the city bus, and pretty soon I'll be able to drive myself."

As he hustled away in the direction of Knownwell High School, Norris's mom did her own eye-roll and sighed. "As if *that's* supposed to make me feel any better . . ."

Norris made his way through the parking lot and across the flag patio toward the three sets of double doors marking the threshold of his journey for the next four years. With each step, a bit of his bravado evaporated, replaced by the slightest twinge of apprehension. And then he heard his name.

"Norris! Hey, man! Over here!" It was the voice of his mentor, an upperclassman he had met two weeks earlier during orientation. Mark was waiting near the center entrance, holding a lanyard in school colors that he dropped ceremoniously over the freshman's head. Pointing to the novelty compass now resting on Norris's chest, he continued the greeting: "You're now a 100 percent official Explorer! Your future is in your hands."

From the orientation meetings, Norris had a sense of how carefully things like colors and symbols and slogans had been chosen. Representatives of the senior class had described how the school began an improvement plan two years earlier that had built on strengths and added new goals and focus. Months of discussion had taken place with staff, alumni, and district administrators just on the issue of a mascot.

Loyalty to a century-old tradition was challenged by sensitivity to the connotation of the previous mascot and its potential impact on the inclusive school culture they wanted to create. Emotions had sometimes flared, but in the end, "Explorer" was chosen to depict students' experiences at Knownwell High School. School colors of red and white with black accents were preserved, enhanced with descriptors. Red was associated with "heart—love and caring." White referred to "clear minds—honesty and integrity." The black accents were meant to represent "detail, definition, identity"—the uniqueness emerging as young men and women found and strengthened their understanding of themselves and their potential. The compass had been chosen to represent every student's ability to shape his or her direction in life.

As Norris nervously unfolded and refolded the schedule he had received at orientation, he remembered it wasn't going to apply on the first day of school. The schedule was being adjusted to provide an extended advisory period. Norris looked again at the list of 16 names. He knew some of them already, because they were ninth graders too. He wondered what it would be like to interact with sophomores, juniors, and seniors. Some of his middle school friends were going to a school where they would be in a separate wing from any other grades.

"Well, let's go meet the rest of our group, Norris. I'm glad you've got your notebook with you—we usually have some time when we write down our thoughts or questions. And you probably have quite a few. Remember that you can speak up on anything, anytime—there's a mutual respect here and us seniors aren't going to intimidate you, . . ." Mark smiles as he adds, ". . . at least not intentionally."

Norris followed his mentor into the classroom, thinking, "I hope they don't realize right away that Morris is my big brother. Everybody seems to think he's a big deal around here. The first question that I want answered is—what did he do anyway?"

Puzzles and Premises

You just met Norris and his mentor, Mark. Norris wants to know why his older brother, Morris, is referred to like a folk hero at Knownwell High School. In these pages, you'll get to know Morris, a thoughtful, slightly geeky kid who was curious about what was going on in his school and began a series of conversations that illuminated the importance of students as stakeholders in our work in schools.

There isn't a real Morris. He represents the many students that I have already met, and that I believe are in our schools, having constructive things to say, waiting to be heard, wanting to be "contributing citizens," wondering how to get their voices into the mix. I chose the name Morris so I could write about "Morris's school," because back in the 1990s, I met Ted Sizer's Horace (Sizer, 1992). Sizer wrote about Horace's school through a teacher's eyes. I hope I can illuminate a school through students' eyes. The comments and insights offered by Morris and his fellow students are not a complete flight of fantasy. They reflect my own experiences with students and schools and are guided by the findings of others who have listened for student voice.

There also isn't one specific place to visit that is Knownwell High School. Just as Horace's school was a semifictionalized prototype, Morris's school is a semifictionalized composite of several real-life settings I have visited, incorporating other personal observations and documented sources. Knownwell High School is imaginary only as the lid of the puzzle box, where all the pieces from multiple examples fit together. Everything described in Morris's life as a student at Knownwell High School has or does exist in reality somewhere. I believe we can put more of the pieces together in more places and increase the momentum toward schools where rigor, relevance, and relationships are the norm, not the exception (Gates, cited in Mundy, 2003).

PUZZLES

My interest in students as stakeholders in schools, especially high schools, arises from a set of puzzles that have intrigued and frustrated me for the past 15 years. Our work at the National Center for Effective Schools was based primarily on studies from elementary schools where student achievement exceeded that of other schools with similar demographic profiles. Finding high school examples was nearly impossible. For that matter, it still is.

Puzzle #1. Why do groups of adults give surveys to students and then sit around trying to figure out what the responses mean from our middle-aged perspectives on life? We see the students every day. We realize that they are living in a different world. Why don't we ask *them,* the actual respondents to the surveys, to help us interpret the results?

Puzzle #2. Why do teachers complain so much about students not taking any responsibility for their learning? For the first 8 or 10 years of their school experience, we succumb to the temptation to take all the responsibility ourselves. We define all the details for them and then wonder why they show so little initiative. How many pages? What font? Where should I put my name? Will it be on the test? I wonder if our *own practices* instill a learned dependence that comes back to bite us later in the form of student apathy.

Puzzle #3. Why are there more books and articles and an increasing research base on student voice and the importance of student engagement—and so few examples of applying those findings and engaging students in the real work of the school?

Puzzle #4. Is Bill Gates right? Is the only way to change high schools a matter of creating a lot of smaller ones? Is structure the only barrier to personalization, engagement, and responsibility? Does even Bill have enough bills to support enough small schools and provide the resources they require? What of a district like Marysville, Washington, with a high school of 2,300 scattered in multiple buildings—some permanent, some portable—in a community that hasn't passed a construction bond issue since 1990? What can an ordinary high school do with its existing resources and limited community support for change?

Puzzle #5. While we're focusing on providing every student with the prerequisite skills for postsecondary education, who's looking after the funding to create more room in higher education institutions for this cohort of "everybody to college" high school graduates?

Puzzle #6. Since political and corporate minds started making education policy that focuses narrowly on reading and math, who's paying attention to "the whole child"?

Puzzle #7. Why are schools putting things into mission statements like "becoming contributing members of society" and "productive citizens in a global economy" and "lifelong learner" but not granting full participation in the immediate society around them—their school community?

Puzzle #8. When I'm feeling so passionate about authentic student engagement in schoolwide improvement and their individual learning, why do I have to rewrite so much of *my own text* to make it consistent with my purpose? In my first draft of Norris's entry to Knownwell High School, I had him picking up his mandatory photo ID and clipping it to his regulation lanyard—revealing the limitations and inconsistencies of my own mental models (Senge, 1990).

PREMISES

If any of these puzzles are shared and merit attention, then surely there must be alternatives and solutions. These solutions must be feasible with relatively the same resources. Even the most generous philanthropic contributions have an expiration date. They are only seed money. If what is grown from the seed cannot continue to be propagated, nurtured, sustained, and replicated, the one-time improvements only contribute to doubts and reluctance to engage in other major efforts in the future. My premise is that there *are* answers and that *students* can help us find them.

Premise #1. The American high school is the last laboratory in which students can engage in "guided practice" of democracy, citizenship, and individual responsibility. As such, students can and should be true stakeholders in planning and problem solving within their immediate community, the school. This happens in Morris's school, and I believe it can happen in yours.

Premise #2. Schools can be more personalized and students more engaged if the adults aren't trying to do all the work. Students can be taught how to help, even with professional challenges like differentiated instruction.

Premise #3. Very few school districts have been able to sell and sustain support for major restructuring efforts in high schools. I premise that our mental models represent thicker walls and boxes to break down than the physical structures of our schools. That's why Morris's school is a rather traditional place, not broken into schools-within-a-school or academies. I raise the possibility that changes in time and relationships can occur within fairly typical high school settings.

Premise #4. Students can be visionaries, advocates, and change agents—when given the permission, the expectation, and some guidance. It is not so much whether students have the courage to face the challenges as it is whether we have the courage to hear their voices and let their energy pull us to think outside the boxes of our experience and training. Perhaps we have run out of creativity or energy or hope. Perhaps instead of feeling that we must instill those characteristics *into* the young, we can draw theirs *out* and be revitalized in the process.

So, how did this engagement of students as stakeholders begin at Knownwell High School?

September, Year 1

Morris, Mr. Spark, and the Table Ten Advisory Group

It's lunchtime, and the Commons is teeming with students. Mr. Spark and the assistant principals cruise the area, greeting students, sliding chairs back into vacant spaces at tables, occasionally picking up litter left behind from the previous shift. Amid the din, they issue softly spoken reminders of expectations and congratulate team members on Friday night's victory.

As Mr. Spark moves away from the tables and heads toward the office, Morris shuffles over. His jeans drag on the ground, he looks sideways and clears his throat as he shoves his glasses back up onto the bridge of his nose. "Uh, Mr. Spark, can I, um, ask you about something?"

"Sure, Morris. What's on your mind?"

"Well, I heard some teachers talking in the hall about accreditation, and I just wondered about that. Like, uh, we wouldn't have trouble getting into college from here or anything, would we?"

"Not to worry, Morris. We already have accreditation, and it's just something we have to do every few years. We get some stuff put together for some people to come visit, and we get our accreditation renewed. It happens in all high schools."

"Oh, well, that's good then. About our school being good enough so we can get into college and all. But why did the teachers sound sorta mad about it?"

"Whoa. I'm not sure what that's all about, Morris. I guess I need you to tell me more. What made you think they were mad?"

"Well, uh, I mean, I don't want to get anybody into trouble or nothing. You know?"

"Yes, Morris. I'm just curious. I want to know what teachers are thinking about. Can you help me a little more?"

"Well, OK then. I think they were saying that they have to do an improvement plan and it will take a lot of time and they think the school is just fine already and why have a bunch more meetings—like that. You know?"

"I see. Well, Morris, I guess I have some work to do. I think improvement is a good thing even if the school is OK already. We can always find ways to be even better. Thanks for sharing this with me."

As Mr. Spark turns to continue on his way, Morris speaks softly one more time. "I, um, I might have some ideas about that, Mr. Spark."

At the moment, Mr. Spark is preoccupied with wondering why his teachers are complaining about the possibility that things could be improved in some way, and irritated that they are talking that way in earshot of the students. He overhears Morris's last comment but doesn't pick up on it right away.

At dismissal time, Morris knows Mr. Spark will be near the door watching students depart. Somewhat embarrassed by his boldness at lunchtime, he heads for the far door and is surprised when Mr. Spark calls out his name. "Morris, you said you had some ideas about our school. Would you talk with me some more about that at lunch tomorrow?" Morris nods, shifts his stack of books, and shuffles out the door.

The next day, Mr. Spark finds Morris seated at a lunch table with an unlikely assortment of students from the junior class. Mr. Spark recognizes that two of them are students he recently discussed in IEP meetings. Another is a young man he has chastised several times for skateboarding on the patio. And he's most intrigued by the presence of a Goth, all in black, including lipstick. "Hi, Morris. I was curious about what you said yesterday about ideas for our school. What's on your mind?"

"Well, Mr. Spark, I was wondering what all this accreditation and school improvement stuff is about. And we, um, well, we kinda wonder if it's about all of us kids or just, um, well, just if it's really about everybody."

"Morris, did you get this table together on purpose? Are you trying to tell me that you're not sure if this school is for you?"

"Well, we kinda know each other because we all have to take the regular school lunch and we see each other in that, uh, line for . . . Well, anyway, you did say you were interested. And, uh, there's, like, this leadership class in school, but, uh, nobody like us is on it, so we thought maybe we could just sort of talk to you once in a while. What's supposed to be happening in this school improvement thing?"

"Well, there will be a school improvement team, and it's supposed to have representatives of our stakeholders on it—people who have a stake in the school, like the administration and teachers, and there will be parents and businesspeople and someone from the university. They have a bunch of things to do, like develop a Mission Statement and analyze data and set goals and pick strategies to make the school better. Is that what you wanted to know?"

"Well, Mr. Spark, what we really wanted to know is—since we go here every day and all—we were kind of wondering, that is, no disrespect or anything, but, um, would you think that maybe we are stakeholders too?"

Stunned into silence, Mr. Spark can only nod. And the unofficial, ad hoc Table Ten Advisory Group is born.

QUESTIONS FOR REFLECTION

1. The change process at Knownwell High School was prompted by the external mandate of school accreditation. What precipitating events—internal or external—could provide leverage to begin a change process in your school?

2. On his first day at Knownwell High School, Norris was greeted with colors and symbols carefully selected by the students to convey the school culture. What colors, symbols, and slogans convey the culture of your school? How were they chosen? Would it make a difference if students were the ones to communicate their meaning and message?

3. How do staff members talk in front of students in your school? Would they be surprised to know what students hear and conclude?

4. Mr. Spark's first comments about the school improvement team did not include students. Why might that be true? Is it conscious or unconscious? When you thought about students as stakeholders, which students came to mind first? Why?

5. As you answer these questions in your own mind, what will you do to check the accuracy of your perceptions with students?

CONTENT FOR CONSIDERATION

Breaking Ranks II is a publication of the National Association of Secondary School Principals (NASSP) (2004) that has become the Rand McNally atlas of high school reform. Among its recommendations for "changing an American institution" is Cornerstone 6—Distributed Leadership. "Institute structural leadership changes that allow for meaningful involvement in decision making by students, teachers, family members, and the community and that support effective communication with these groups" (p. 13). Actions that would support this strategy include (a) formalizing participation in site-based decision-making teams, school leadership councils, strategic planning and school improvement teams and (b) providing student government and other leadership forums with opportunities to be included in discussions of substantive issues. Quoting the original *Breaking Ranks* (NASSP, 1996) document, leaders are reminded that there is "merit in including students on various committees that determine policies that affect discipline, grading standards, and participation on sports teams. A high school that follows such a philosophy will do all it can, for example, to foster a viable student government. It will also convene forums in which students can share ideas about school reform. . . . Young people learn how to exercise responsibility by having the chance to do so" (p. 32).

Earlier descriptions of the "productive" high school (Murphy, Beck, Crawford, Hodges, & McGaughy, 2001) also emphasized student involvement in decision making, urging schools to "accord students both more power and more responsibility. . . . Everyone involved with schools—students, teachers, and administrators—will need to view students differently. The student voice will have to be acknowledged" (McQuillan, cited in Murphy et al., 2001).

Other writers agreed that "[e]ffective high schools find ways to give students legitimate voice in academic areas, policy decisions, school organization, discipline, and activities (Bobbett & French, 1992; Mackin, 1996; Meier, 1995; Ogden & Germinario, 1995). . . . Using advisory groups, tutorial settings, honor councils, one-on-one meetings with staff, and student forums, schools gain input on how things are going at the school and what suggestions for change the students might have (Duke, 1995; McQuillan, 1995; Raywid, 1995; Shore, 1995)" (Murphy et al., 2001).

A STUDENT GETS THE LAST WORD

As schools move to elicit and respond to student voice, a student warns that there is not just one voice to be heard.

> When you do involve students, don't just go to the student council or the "top" students. They represent just one group. Maybe the students you really need to talk to are the ones who are ditching. The main point is to talk to as many students as possible. (What Kids Can Do, n.d.)

Students as Stakeholders

4

This past summer, I was honored by Corwin Press for having achieved a milestone in sales through four books I have written on school change and improvement. In each of them, I referred to *stakeholders*. I defined the term this way:

> The people we're talking about are the full range of interested parties frequently called *stakeholders*. The school improvement process should be open and participatory, involving teachers, administrators, support staff, students, parents, community representatives, and business partners in a variety of ways. For convenience, I use two inclusive terms. The word *staff* refers to all the adults who work in the school, whether they are licensed teachers, aides, clerical support, or administrators. The term *constituents* refers to the interested adult parties outside the school, including parents and community members. Students belong in a category by themselves. They are the most intimately involved with and aware of the school's needs and successes—at the same time that they are least integrated into analysis, decision-making, and planning processes. (Holcomb, 2004, p. 39)

There it is, in my own words: students are the most intimately involved, aware, affected, and least integrated. And then I droned on for another 227 pages, describing almost exclusively the roles of school and district staff, leaving the students' voice silent yet again.

CREATING THE SPACE FOR ACTIVE STUDENT VOICE

Literature that does include student voice consists primarily of results from surveys, focus groups, and interviews that describe what students think should be changed in the future or their reactions to new programs or practices after they have been put in place. In the first case, there is little sense of how the student input gets used. In the second, it's rarely clear whether student voice helped to shape the innovation that's being declared a success.

I would characterize this as relatively passive student voice, with students as data sources. What I want to see is active use of student voice in an ongoing way—to shape school plans before, during, and after. Perhaps the student voice is "passive" because it occurs as an event, rather than a process. When it's an event—"Let's get some survey data for our portfolio"— there's no place for it to go except into the data bank. There must be a place, a space, a structure to *keep* engaging, acting on, and broadcasting the student voice. I believe that space is in the school's ongoing decision-making and improvement process. This chapter provides an overview of school improvement processes as a framework for authentic student engagement in the practice of democracy and the realities of accountability. The last section, Untapped Potential: Students as Stakeholders, and Figure 4.4 highlight the specific roles of students as stakeholders.

THE SCHOOL IMPROVEMENT PROCESS

Figure 4.1 is a composite of the key components from a variety of change processes used in school districts I have known: Effective Schools models, school accreditation processes, total quality management, strategic planning, and most recently, school improvement plans required by state accountability systems and demanded by the No Child Left Behind reauthorization of the Elementary and Secondary Education Act. Although I have frequently seen one or two of these components done well, I have rarely seen a fully aligned system. But I have observed that the districts with the most tightly aligned and data-driven approaches to change and improvement are also those making a difference in student achievement. The visual organizer of an aligned achievement plan appears three times in this chapter. First, we explore the relationships between the components and their related action plans (Figures 4.1 and 4.2). Then we describe the essential uses of data at critical points in the school improvement process (Figure 4.3). Finally, we revisit the essential components of school decision making with a focus on students' roles as authentic stakeholders in their school community (Figure 4.4).

Figure 4.1 The School Improvement Process

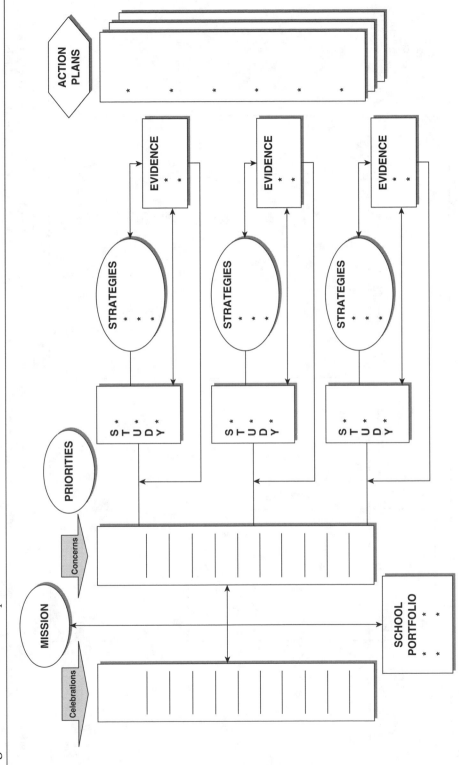

Figure 4.2   Action Plan Form

Activities: Steps to Be Taken	Persons Responsible	Persons Involved	Resources Needed	Timeline	Monitoring— Evidence of Implementation & Impact

Alignment Between Mission and the School Portfolio

The literature on change strongly emphasizes the importance of an organization articulating its core values and purposes in a statement or document that guides planning and problem solving. I believe that the mission is also a set of commitments for which the organization is accountable. The vertical arrow between the Mission and the School Portfolio demonstrates the need to provide evidence that the mission is being fulfilled.

The term *School Portfolio* is used here to describe a collection of data compiled at the individual school level. Data are gathered about student achievement, other student characteristics, staff and program characteristics, and parent/community characteristics and satisfaction. Multiple data sources include large-scale standardized assessment data as well as more formative, local indicators of student learning. Existing sources of data include records kept on attendance, behavior, and graduation rates. Objective data are balanced with perceptual data from surveys, interviews, and focus groups with stakeholders, including students, staff, administrators, and family and community members.

Alignment Between Mission, Portfolio, Celebrations, and Concerns

The data assembled in the School Portfolio provide schools with an opportunity to describe the wide variety of needs it addresses, highlight examples of success to celebrate, and demonstrate evidence of improvement occurring where needed. Celebrations are critical in maintaining a culture of hope, energy, and motivation in the midst of a sense of urgency for change.

The relationship between the Mission and the School Portfolio is that one should provide evidence of the other. We must check for alignment between our "espoused theories" (Argyris & Schön, 1974) and our "theories in use" (how we operate on a daily basis). When we provide evidence of what we do, how closely does it match what we say? Our integrity is judged by whether "we do what we say we will do."

The length of the vertical arrow between Mission and School Portfolio represents the amount of consistency or discrepancy between rhetoric and reality. Awareness of this discrepancy should generate a range of concerns, which Peter Senge (1990) might describe as "creative tension." The horizontal arrow emphasizes that the *concerns* a school plans to address should arise directly from the values they hold dear and the data they examine courageously.

Alignment Between Concerns and Priorities

If the school portfolio includes a variety of data from a range of sources, many concerns may be identified. Only a few can be addressed with the substantive, systemic effort needed to change student achievement. The contrast between many lines in the Concerns box and only three spaces for Priorities represents the need to focus on a few areas of critical importance and major impact on student life and learning.

Alignment Between Priorities, Study, and Strategies

Too often, participants in a school improvement process have unrealistic time expectations placed on them. They may be asked to set new annual goals each year and be given one day to go on retreat and develop the improvement plan. This typical model yields several unintended, undesired consequences. Significant needs are not addressed as goals, because they can't be attained in one year. Strategies for meeting the goals are brainstormed based on the particular experiences and preferences of the group. Important factors in the local context that would inform these decisions are ignored. The three bullet points in the Study component emphasize the necessity for deeper analysis of the data, thorough examination of research and best practice, and honest analysis of existing practices within the school. Annual plans must be replaced by multiyear plans, with months of planning time provided for thorough work and adequate engagement of those who will be affected by coming changes. The strategies selected for implementation must be consistent with the school's mission, linked to needs arising from data, and proven effective in other settings. There are three bullets in the oval labeled Strategies, but they do not represent three specific tasks as the three bullets in the Study box do. They serve as a reminder that there *is no* single silver bullet or magic potion/program that can solve a complex problem. A powerful combination of effective strategies must be created and coordinated.

Alignment Between Priorities, Strategies, and Evidence

Traditional methods of program evaluation and school improvement have claimed success by reporting evidence that selected strategies were implemented. Glowing accounts are provided of the number of teachers who attended training and the number of new initiatives begun. We often reported just what the adults did, rather than the results achieved for students, because that is what we *knew how* to do. Individual teachers kept track of students' progress in idiosyncratic ways at the classroom level, but there was little assurance that this data matched schoolwide goals or could be aggregated to show student progress for the school as a whole. High-performing schools (Shannon & Bylsma, 2003) identify formative assessments they will use to monitor students in a more frequent, more authentic, and less threatening way than the large-scale assessments they also administer and analyze. The two bullet points in the Evidence component of Figure 4.1 represent the need to verify *implementation* of the selected strategies and ensure that this effort has an *impact* on student learning.

The arrows that go back and forth and around Priorities, Strategies, and Evidence illustrate that this is cyclical, continuous, ongoing work. The process is not as straightforward as the two-dimensional confines of print make it appear. For example, the two-way arrow between Strategies and Evidence reminds us that determining what evidence we need and learning how to gather it will also inform what we need to do as strategies so the evidence we seek will be available. Final decisions about strategies should not be made until after discussion of what goal attainment would look like and how that would be documented. The two-way arrow between Evidence and Study illustrates the eventuality that if those strategies do not yield the needed results, its back to the study phase to reassess and revise the plan.

Alignment Between Strategies, Evidence, and Action Plans

The components of Mission, School Portfolio, Priorities, Strategies, and Evidence in Figure 4.1 represent the major components of a change or improvement plan. They signal major decisions about what the school's focus will be, what new work the school will initiate, and how the school will determine its effectiveness. This overall "plan-at-a-glance" can be displayed, publicized, and referred to frequently. Figures 22.1 through 22.7 illustrate how this visual display would evolve over time. This big picture view helps keep leaders, staff, and stakeholders grounded when multiple efforts seem overwhelming and they may feel that things are starting to spin out of control.

The overall plan describes why (mission and portfolio), what (goals), and how (strategies and evidence). When it comes to putting all this work into place, school leaders need more specific, concrete action plans to identify who, when, where, and with what funding. The Action Plan blocks in Figures 4.1, 4.3, and 4.4 are a reminder that more detailed planning is needed to ensure implementation of the strategies that were selected and collection of the needed evidence to document success. The headings on Figure 4.2 capture the detailed planning that will be monitored to provide evidence of implementation and impact.

USE OF DATA TO GUIDE DECISION MAKING

An essential tool for aligning a school's efforts to increase student achievement is data. In Figure 4.3, the word *data* has been superimposed at critical points on the basic diagram from Figure 4.1. More detailed descriptions and examples of data use at each stage are provided in *Getting Excited About Data: Combining People, Passion, and Proof to Maximize Student Achievement* (Holcomb, 2004).

Data for Initial Review

The initial version of the School Portfolio is clarified as baseline data. Schools begin to gather information about (a) student achievement, (b) student characteristics and perceptions, (c) staff characteristics, practices,

20

Figure 4.3   Critical Points for the Use of Data in the School Improvement Process

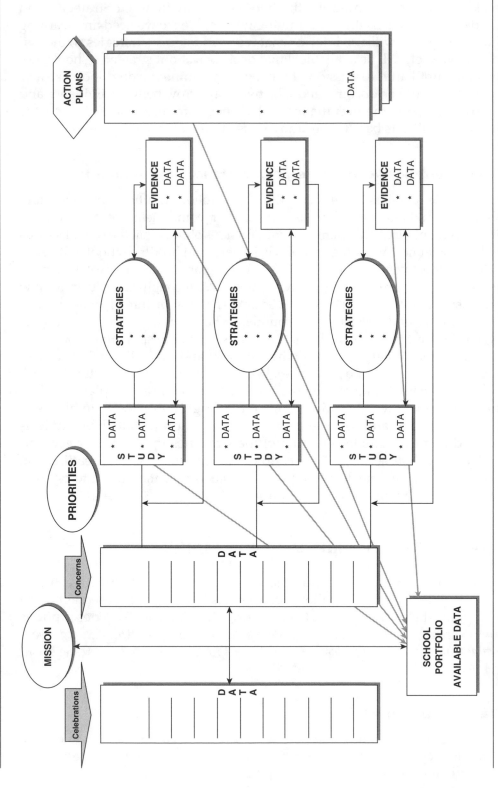

and perceptions, and (d) community characteristics and perceptions. Once people begin to discover what they *could* include in the initial School Portfolio, it becomes a challenge to limit its size and scope. Shaded arrows have been added to illustrate how the school's data portfolio continually expands as more data are acquired and used throughout the process. Since the School Portfolio is a work in progress at all times, there will be ample opportunities to add more information or more detailed analysis as the process continues. The arrows in Figure 4.3 emphasize how the use of data is not a one-time event in a linear process but an ongoing practice in a continuous improvement cycle.

Data to Focus Priorities

Data must be used as a filter to help the school focus on a limited number of priority areas (Shannon & Bylsma, 2003). This is critical, because it creates a linkage that will strengthen the school's capacity to deal with implementation problems later on. When changes in practice and addition of new strategies become difficult, the "Why are we doing this?" question will surface from participants. The best answers to the why question come from clear connections back to the data that demonstrate the need and to the mission and values that motivate the stakeholders in the school.

Data From Further Study

The three bullets in the Study box represent further analysis of the data related to each priority issue or need, investigation of best practices, and review of current programs and instructional practices. When new strategies are being considered, data that substantiate their claims of effectiveness must be a prerequisite. Data on current practice might include documenting and comparing the amount of time each teacher devotes to an essential skill or standard revealed as a concern in the student achievement data. The shaded arrow shows how these data become part of the School Portfolio as it is continually updated.

Data to Document Results

As improvement goals are crafted into language that will motivate whole-school effort, the question, "How will we know we're getting there?" should be raised. Some answers will be very evident, because there are data sources that were already available and were used in the initial School Portfolio that can be monitored over time. Standardized tests and state assessments are two examples. Other answers will have to be constructed as professionals discuss what could be measured, observed, or aggregated from information they already keep as individual teachers.

Plans for Ongoing Data Collection

A school's completed version of Figure 4.1 would identify the data that will be used to document progress. Some of this will be test data that automatically come from the state to the district and on to the school. Other data will be school specific and must be intentionally collected. The plans for this data collection should be embedded in the Action Plans. If we don't plan ahead and take the action needed to get the proof of our efforts, we can easily become discouraged and lose credibility.

UNTAPPED POTENTIAL: STUDENTS AS STAKEHOLDERS

This chapter introduced Figures 4.1 and 4.3 to illustrate the components of school planning, emphasizing how they must be internally aligned and informed by use of data to maximize impact on student learning. Figure 4.4 presents another image of this process of school decision making. In this figure, the word *students* has been embedded to highlight the many ways in which students have the potential to shape schools for learning and community life. This book recommends full engagement of students at these crucial points:

- Developing and affirming the school's mission and beliefs
- Identifying significant, meaningful data to be compiled for decision making
- Interpreting the data, identifying additional data, and identifying areas of concern
- Focusing areas of concern to a few priorities
- Participating in study groups to further analyze data in priority areas and recommend strategies
- Affirming the completed improvement plan
- Participating in implementation of new strategies and assessments
- Documenting and discussing evidence of implementation and impact of the chosen strategies

Students as Stakeholders in the School Culture

Peterson and Deal have defined school culture as the "underlying set of norms, values, beliefs, rituals and traditions that make up the unwritten rules of how to think, feel and act in an organization" (Peterson, cited in Sizer, n.d.). They describe unwritten rules for almost anything that goes on in a school, including decision making: Who is involved? And how? These unwritten rules are often unconscious—so the question of whether students are stakeholders and how they may be engaged must be brought to the surface.

Figure 4.4 Students as Stakeholders in the School Improvement Process

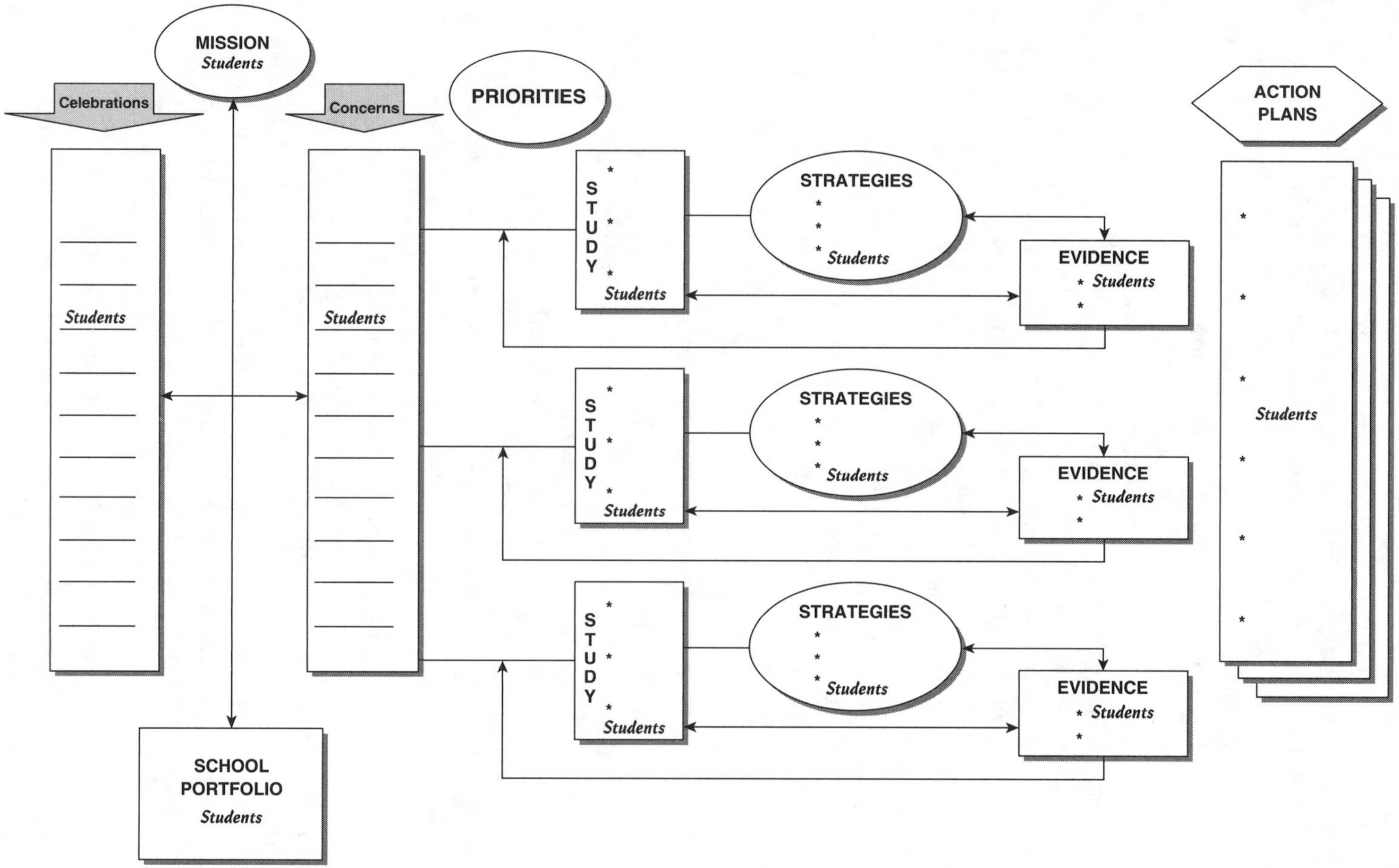

The culture of the school is shaped through and characterized by prevailing norms and values, heroes and stories, and rites and rituals. Whether they are intentionally created or evolve incidentally through events and the passage of time, these elements are present in every school. Development of mission statements is one way in which schools seek to articulate desired beliefs. Students should be active participants in the process of identifying the mission, critiquing it, and analyzing how well it is actualized by staff and students in the school.

As early as the 1970s, a safe, orderly environment and a climate of high expectations for student success were identified among the characteristics of schools considered effective because their students outperformed those in similar settings (Holcomb, 1991). In the 1990s, school shootings and increased incidence (and/or keener awareness) of threats and bullying increased attention on the need to feel safe at school. Studies in search of schools with answers on how to close the achievement gap reemphasized students' needs to feel that they are special, cared about, and believed in (Johnson, 2002).

At Knownwell High School, Norris experienced a first-day ritual (Chapter 3) designed by students and infused with intentional symbolism. He will learn more about the role Morris and his fellow students played in development of the norms that pervade the culture of his school.

Students as Stakeholders in Use of Data

Like most states, the academic standards for the state of Washington set expectations that students will "understand and apply data collection methods to obtain the desired information" (Washington OSPI, 2004a, p. 33)—and that's for students in Grade 4. Fifth graders are expected to "apply strategies to organize, display and interpret data" (p. 36).

One of the challenges often faced by school improvement teams is the need to transform rows and columns of numbers into graphs and other formats that will provide useful and user-friendly information for decision making. Students have the time and need the practice. Enlist their help.

Students are a valuable source of data, through surveys, focus groups, and interviews. They can also gather data, conducting focus groups and interviews as follow-up to the general survey traditionally administered every few years to staff, students, and parents. And as Morris points out in Chapter 6, their voice is essential to clarify and challenge adult interpretations and analyses of student responses.

Students as Stakeholders Planning for Change

When school improvement teams are engaged in the study of best practices and programs, students can also research the same topics and compare findings and recommendations. Adults who ponder how to engage and motivate students would do well to look around, find an assortment of those who are successful, those who struggle, and those who are disengaged, and ask them what it would take to push them to do their best work or to become involved in improving their school.

Students as Stakeholders Monitoring Change

Students are amazingly patient with teachers who are trying new practices and legitimately frustrated with those who won't. When school improvement plans identify how they will know that things are changing, students can provide valuable insights on those indicators.

Students as Stakeholders in Ongoing Issues

The school board was deadlocked. I was there in my role as a district administrator. The issue was whether to approach the voters with a referendum to enlarge the high school. Various speakers came to the podium to speak for and against the issue. Most had individual interests that were self-evident: the senior citizens fearing new taxes, the property owners across the street from the high school fearing new traffic, the teachers demanding better working conditions. A member of the student council approached the podium and asked to show a short video she and her classmates had filmed during passing periods as students jammed the halls. She pleaded with the board to at least give voters the chance to have their say. After a smattering of applause, the board president said, "Young lady, we pretty much know before they start what people will say and why. But you are graduating and won't be here. You came through the current high school very well. What is your interest in this issue?" Very respectfully she looked him in the eye and said, "I have two younger brothers. I just want them to have a better place than I did." The room became very silent. Within minutes, the board voted to put the issue before the voters, and shortly thereafter, the voters granted the young lady's wish.

If schools undertake to create citizens, they should engage students in the practice of democracy within the society of the school. Teachers need not rack their brains for ways to create relevancy. The relevancy surrounds the students all the time. They just need the opportunity to engage with it.

Students as Stakeholders at Any Age

Morris's school is a high school, but the concept of students as stakeholders should not be limited to those in Grades 9–12. Insights offered by elementary and middle school students can be astounding. Years ago, I called my niece Kacie to ask about her first day of kindergarten. She told me about her class. "We have 13 boys and only 7 girls. That's not going to work out very well when we get older and start getting married." She told me about her teacher. "I think she's probably nice in real life, but I can tell she has to be pretty crabby until she gets all those boys in line." She gave me her philosophy about learning. "There's just one thing wrong, Aunt Edie. I'm afraid the teacher's not very flexible." I asked for clarification. "Remember we went shopping and got that school box and put all that stuff in it that we need to use for learning things? Well, the teacher says we have to leave it in our cubby every night and not take it home. Doesn't she think I might want to learn something at home?"

October, Year 1

Sentiments on Surveys, Morris on (a) Mission, and Joe Meets Mo

"So, Mr. Spark, what's happening with that accreditation stuff that's supposed to improve our school? You know, Mission Statement and all that." The principal leans against the lunch table in the busy Commons area and sets aside the handful of collected debris from departing diners.

"I guess I haven't talked with you for a few days, and it's time for an update, isn't it, Morris? We've had a consultant come in and meet with the school improvement team. He checked to be sure we have a lot of people represented on the team. You'll be glad to know there are student representatives included. Joe's there. You know him, right? President of the student body? And Jane's there from Student Senate."

"So there's just two and they're both seniors. Are they the only ones? Do we get to put in any ideas?"

"Morris, you have a very good point. I'm going to do a couple of things. First, I'm going to make sure I hook you up with Joe. I've put a lot of work into our culture here, and I want to make sure that people in leadership roles remember that they represent everybody. And I'm going to work on some ways to tap into lots of student ideas as we're working on our status report and school improvement plan. Do you have some ideas about how I could do that?"

"Well, one thing you could do is let everybody know this is going on. Like when you do daily greetings on the intercom. Then people could start thinking about it. And you could have the leadership people hook up with some groups for discussion—like at lunch or after school. Maybe teachers could give up a few minutes in homeroom, or some teachers could have a topic in class if it would fit."

"Those are good ideas, Morris. I'm going to add them to my plans. The consultant also said that we would have a survey to use. It has a form for staff and parents and students to fill out. So that will be a chance for every student to respond. I hope you'll encourage your friends to take it seriously and answer honestly."

So far, the rest of the unofficial ad hoc Table Ten Advisory Group had been silent. At the mention of a survey, more voices chimed in.

"Mr. Spark, it has to be short. I need extra time to read, and I won't be able to answer it all if it's too long."

"How are you going to know what we really mean when we answer the questions? Or are you just going to go with numbers and average them out?"

"We already did one survey, and it was super long, and it asked us all about if we do drugs and have sex and go to church and stuff like that. Whatever happened from that survey? Is this going to be the same thing?"

Mr. Spark smiled as he sensed the energy and interest of this group of young people some would call "disengaged" from the mainstream culture of the school. "That was a different type of survey. Its purpose was to give us an idea of how much at-risk behavior is going on with our kids and what kinds of support they have to keep them physically and emotionally healthy. We will be looking at the results from that survey as one of the data sources when we put together our School Portfolio and decide what we're strong on and what we need to work on."

"So, how is this other survey going to be different?"

"Well, it won't be focused on each individual student and the things you do in your individual lives. It will be about the school and what you think is good about our school and what we could do to make it better. I'm curious to find out whether teachers and parents and students have the same ideas or different ideas about our school. What would you predict?"

"Well . . . you really want to know? I can't get in any trouble, can I?"

"C'mon, Morris, we've known each other for over two years now. Do you think I'm a 'don't get mad, get even' kind of guy?"

"No, Mr. Spark, you're for real. So—here's my prediction. The teachers and the A students will say the school is great. The parents will say you're not strict enough. And most of the students will say we need more help learning."

"Wow. Morris, thanks for being so honest. You have made me very curious and very determined to find out whether you're right. And you've made me realize that I'll need a way to sort out the student data. Otherwise, I won't know whether you're right about different ideas coming from different groups of kids. You just made my work a little harder, but it will turn out a lot better. Thanks, kids. Anything else on your minds?"

"Uh, yeah. You said something about a Mission Statement for the school. What would be the point of that?"

"The consultant went over that with us when he was here. We asked him about it because we've had a Mission Statement before and we weren't sure if it would be a good use of time to do it again."

"Really—there's a Mission Statement? What is it? And what's it for?"

Mr. Spark laughed sheepishly. "You know, Morris, that's the exact same question the teachers asked me. It was kind of embarrassing. The consultant said we obviously have work to do if we don't even know what it is. First we're going to look at the Mission Statement we wrote a few years ago and see if it really captures what we believe. Then we'll know if we should just revise it, or start all over. And we'll also have to reflect on why it just sat there and we forgot about it. Because a Mission Statement is *supposed* to be something we think about all the time. It's our beliefs, and we need to make sure we're living up to our beliefs. Tell you what. I'm making copies of it for the faculty meeting, and I'll stick a copy in my pocket and show you next lunch period, OK?"

"Cool. See you tomorrow, Mr. Spark."

"Hey, Morris. I brought you a copy of that Mission Statement we were talking about the other day. I just got paged, so I have to check on this call, but take a look at it and see what you think. I'll get right back to you." As Mr. Spark moved away, five heads converged above the single sheet of paper in the middle of the table.

> The mission of Knownwell High School is to provide a rigorous curriculum in a supportive and mutually respectful environment that encourages all of its diverse students to succeed academically, producing high quality work, while becoming analytical thinkers and responsible citizens.

"Ooh. Sounds kinda preachy, doesn't it?"

"More like—sounds hypocritical. I mean, Mr. Spark treats us great, but lots of the teachers act like we're morons just because we have an IEP."

"Yeah—what's with 'mutually respectful'? Wouldn't that mean adults respect kids as much as they expect kids to respect them? Wouldn't that mean the regular kids pay a little respect to the geeks and the hangouts too?"

"Well . . . who knew. Like what are we in this thing—the 'diverse students' or the 'analytical thinkers'? Yeah, right."

"Whoa, take it easy, you guys. Mr. Spark is going to ask us what we think about this Mission Statement. What are we going to say?"

"Ooh, that's harsh, Morris. But you're right. We asked for it and now we have to say something. Do you think he really wants the truth?"

"Well, he brought it to us, didn't he? He didn't have to. He could have just blown it off and, like, just sort of kept forgetting to bring it out here to lunch. I think he's serious. Besides, what have we got to lose? We're not exactly the in-crowd here anyway."

"Hey, Morris. Sorry I got called back into the office yesterday and didn't get to talk more with you. Did you guys look at the Mission Statement? What do you think? How does it sound? Should we go back to the drawing board?"

"Well, uh, first we need to check something out. Like—what would happen if we didn't think it was so good? I mean, we know *you* want our ideas, and we trust you. But are you going to tell anybody else? What could happen in our classes? We're not quite the aces there, you know."

"Well, first of all, let me tell you that I think you *could* be aceing your classes. If you're not, I think it's partly something about you and your attitudes and beliefs and it's partly something about how we handle things as a school and in the classrooms. I feel bad right off the bat if you have any fear about what could happen in classes. I want to hear your thoughts, and I may need to pass them along so we can do the best possible work. But if you get any feeling that your input is hurting you in any way, I need to know that too. I would expect you to tell me. Deal?"

Morris looks around the group and does a nonverbal analysis of consensus. "OK, deal. We think this Mission Statement sounds like something you'd hear in church or from some politician on TV. We want to believe it. But we don't really. But, like, we don't want to hurt your feelings or anything."

"It's OK. I can handle that, Morris. Give me some specific examples of what you want to believe and why you don't really think it's true."

"Well, no offense, Mr. Spark, but this is what we think. It says that there will be a rigorous curriculum. That's probably what colleges want and all. But do you know that some teachers act like they should have such a tough grading system and give such ridiculous tests that half of the kids can't handle it. There's some that say, 'I have my standards and if you can't cut it . . .' Sort of a 'my way or the highway' deal. They almost act like they think it proves they're a good teacher if kids drop their class or get D's and F's. So maybe you should explain more what rigorous curriculum means.

"And the part about 'mutually respectful.' Mr. Spark, does 'mutually' mean like how we're talking right now? I mean, we're not being rude, but we're sort of disagreeing with you, and you're not getting all offended. You might not think we're right, but you're still listening to us. I think that's mutually respectful but it doesn't happen with everybody here."

"Do you mean that you feel disrespected by your teachers?"

"Well, duh . . . oops, yes, sir, that's just what I mean. Some of them figure we don't look the way they think we should look, so obviously we probably can't think or learn either. And they give themselves an easy out right there. I mean 'encourages' students to succeed. Like they can just give us this big pep talk and that's it. How about *helping* us succeed. That would be pretty sweet, wouldn't it?"

"And what's being a responsible citizen. Is it just sucking up? Or is it like now, when we really want to help our school be a better place?"

"And . . . Mr. Spark . . . I can pretty much handle when adults don't really understand and respect us. But . . . do you think this Mission Statement would mean anything about how other kids treat us? There's cliques and stuff. And comments. I mean, you might call us your advisory group at Table Ten. That's cool—but they call us the loser's table."

"It's not your fault, though. We know you wouldn't want that. But you can't be everywhere. We just think part of this Mission Statement should be about students and what they believe and do—not just the adults."

"You know, Morris, I really agree. And I'm glad I didn't promise not to share this. I don't need to give your names, but I do need to include your thoughts when I meet with the school improvement team. And I'm even more convinced now that I want to hook you up with Joe. He might be what you call the in-group, but I think he's kind of uncomfortable with it also."

"Joe, I'd like you to meet Morris and this really wonderful group of kids that I told you I've been talking with off and on this fall. They shared some powerful perspectives with me when I showed them the Mission Statement we've had hanging around here. I assured them you would want to hear their comments as well. Thanks for taking the last part of your class period to meet them here during lunch. We might be able to do that more often in the future if this works out."

"Sure, my teacher always stops teaching and gives us work time anyway—so no loss to come down here. You said we'd talk about the Mission Statement in the next school improvement meeting, and we're getting various perspectives, right? So, let's hear what you guys are thinking."

Mr. Spark went on his way, chatting with students at other tables and greeting teachers as they moved through the Commons on their way to the staff lounge. Morris began hesitantly, while the others observed Joe with cautious interest. As Joe took notes, nodding and asking clarifying questions, they began to open up and add more comments.

When the bell rang for Table Ten to leave for their next class, Joe summarized. "It sounds like you have some pretty good reasons for questioning that Mission Statement. Sometimes I even feel like student leaders aren't taken seriously. We do stuff like plan Homecoming skits, but we don't get into the really important stuff. This is a good chance for us to change that. Let's do it."

"Morris, we had that school improvement plan meeting, and it was so cool. The teachers really listened to those ideas you had. They decided to keep the Mission Statement sort of the same but change some words around. Plus, they're going to give all of us students a chance to write something of our own—like our beliefs."

The students at Table Ten glanced at each other, careful not to reveal too much reaction to Joe's comment. "Well, how did they change it?"

"They agreed that 'rigorous curriculum' could be taken the wrong way, and they even admitted that 'encourages' students is kind of wimpy. So the latest draft looks like this:

> The mission of Knownwell High School is to provide diverse and challenging learning experiences in a mutually respectful environment and assure that all students master essential skills, produce high quality work, and practice critical thinking and responsible citizenship.

"Really? 'Diverse and challenging learning experiences'? That sounds a lot better. I hope that means other stuff besides lecture, homework, lecture, homework, lecture, homework."

"I see that 'mutually respectful' didn't change. What does that mean? Same-old, same-old?"

"No, Morris, it means they talked about it and they think it should stay in there because it's important and they want it to be true and they're going to work on it. In fact, they said they're going to have some students come in and talk to the school improvement team about how to improve that. So start thinking about what you would want if the situation was ideal."

"Hey, I'd settle for better—doesn't have to be ideal! Like, we know nobody's perfect."

"Joe, how did you get them to put 'assure' in there?! That's almost like a guarantee or something."

"Well, the consultant that comes in to facilitate some of these meetings—he sort of pushed them by asking questions. He'd say, 'Are you *sure*? For *which* students? *All* the time?' He never told them what word to put, but they could tell he thought 'encourages' was wimpy too."

"Looks like they're 'assuring' more stuff too—essential skills, high-quality work, critical thinking, and responsible citizenship."

"Right on. And did you notice it's 'practice' thinking and citizenship? Like now, not just when you graduate and go on to college . . . if you even do."

"How about this?! They changed 'analytical thinking' to 'critical thinking.' What's the difference?"

"Well, Morris, they started talking about something called Bloom's taxonomy because they said it describes thinking at higher levels than just memorizing. One of the kinds of thinking is analysis, but there's three or four more kinds and they didn't want to focus on just one. So they said 'critical thinking' is a broader term."

"Did they—uh—realize that if they really do this, that we—uh—might be critical for real?"

"Oh, I think so. They mentioned that if they put those things in the Mission Statement, they'd have to be sure there's stuff about them in the school improvement plan."

"Awesome. Now we've got two people speaking for us—Joe and Morris. Ha! Joe and Mo. How's that for a team?!"

As Morris and Joe touched palms in a shy high five, the volume of students' voices began to build at Knownwell High School.

QUESTIONS FOR REFLECTION

1. What is the mission of your school? Who knows what it is? Where is it? Would students say the school "walks its talk"?

2. Mr. Spark uses an informal approach to begin to engage students in discussions about their school. Should he be more forceful and mandate student inclusion in all committees? Why? Why not?

3. What do student leaders do in your school? Whose voices are heard—and not heard?

4. Are students ready to speak up in your school? What barriers might need to be addressed? How can you establish trust?

5. As you answer these questions in your own thinking, what will you do to check the accuracy of your perceptions with students?

CONTENT FOR CONSIDERATION

Eight Levels of Student Participation

Adam Fletcher (2003) writes about meaningful student involvement and outlines eight levels of student participation in schools. From lowest to most powerful for learning, they are as follows:

1. Manipulation—adults use students to support their own causes by pretending those causes are inspired by students.

2. Decoration—adults identify causes and make all the decisions about how students will bolster the cause.

3. Tokenism—students appear to be given a voice, but actually have little choice about what they do.

4. Assigned and taught—students are assigned a role, told how, and taught why they should be involved.

5. Consulted and informed—students give advice, are informed about how their input will be used, but are told the outcomes of the adults' decisions.

6. Adult-initiated, shared decisions—adults initiate projects, classes, or activities, but decision making is shared with the students involved.

7. Student-initiated and directed—students initiate and direct the project, with adults involved only in supportive roles.

8. Student-initiated, shared decisions with teachers—projects are initiated by students, with decision making shared among students and adults. These projects empower students while at the same time enabling them to access and learn from the life experience and expertise of adults.

Hawaii's Students Speak

An example that might be considered tokenism is the common practice of designating a student representative to the board of education. Students in Hawaii must feel strongly about whether this is authentic student involvement. When 150 students were gathered for the Hawaii Secondary Student Conference (Serrano, 2005), they began with 71 ideas and reached consensus on nine recommendations to policymakers:

- Make kindergarten mandatory
- Give full voting rights to the board of education student member
- Designate money to relieve the public schools' backlog of school maintenance and repair
- Reconsider the weighted student formula and how each school will be given its money
- Implement a college admissions and financial aid counseling program for graduating high school students
- Increase emphasis on mathematics, science, and social studies to address expectations of the Hawaii State Assessment and the federal No Child Left Behind Act
- Allocate resources to educate Hawaii's youth on drug and illicit substance abuse and treatment for adolescent drug and substance abusers
- Employ a peer counseling program to create unity and safety in Hawaii's public high schools
- Replace external suspension with rehabilitative disciplinary methods for all public schools

These students grappled with tough issues of school finance and facilities, substance abuse, safety and security, and school readiness. True participation of their representative ranks right near the top of their list. They want to be heard at the board level (and since the State of Hawaii is all one school district, this means being heard at the state level). But they are not trying to just get more power. In the same list of priorities, they show willingness to contribute as peer counselors within their schools.

Student Voice Team

In contrast to "token" representation on school boards, an example of the highest level of student involvement might be the new 20-member Student Voice team, which has replaced the traditional student council at Reagan High School in Houston (Richardson, 2004). The Student Voice team meets weekly and works on such questions as whether the school should shift from its current single-lunch schedule to a schedule with multiple lunches, whether students should wear identification badges or uniforms, and what rules should govern backpack use at school. One teacher leads this team, and she is selected by the students.

Principal as Keeper of the Mission

As important as these roles are for teachers, it is the principal who must be the keeper (and shaper) of the school culture. A mission statement is a valuable tool to guide this work, capturing in words the core values of the school. In one setting, a huge bulletin board in the school foyer was set up with the components presented in Figure 4.1. Staff members created a beautiful poster of their mission statement and displayed it on the top left corner of the bulletin board. In the lower left corner, they posted the executive summary of their conclusions from analysis of the data in their school portfolio. The priority goals they set were lettered in calligraphy on strips of chart paper. Strategies for each goal were connected by strings of yarn, which gave them the ability to connect several strategies to more than one goal area. The combined master plan was illustrated with a series of laminated monthly calendars that highlighted the events from their action plans. Any visitor to the school knew what was happening and why. Any new idea had to pass the acid test of proving where it would fit on that crowded, colorful bulletin board. This visual proof of focus is one way of reinforcing the desired culture of the school and operationalizing the mission statement (Holcomb, 2004).

A STUDENT GETS THE LAST WORD

I clearly recall one spring when a middle school principal was on medical leave and I was one of the central office administrators providing support with critical tasks—like lunchroom duty. It was a fascinating opportunity to ask students about their school, and one day I made "mission" my mission. I asked several students what they thought the mission of the school was. The first few were very suave in assuring me that the mission of a school is to "teach us kids." The fourth response was much more fascinating. "Well, if you want to know the real truth, I'm thinking that the mission of the school is probably soccer." When asked to elaborate, he continued, "Well, it's really easy to get out of class for soccer practice and games. But there's absolutely no way to get out of a soccer practice to get some help with your math. So I'm guessing soccer is the most important thing here."

November, Year 1

Morris Does Data

"Hey, Mr. Spark! That was cool on the intercom today—how you told everybody about school improvement and talked about the Mission. I can't believe you're really going to spend the whole week talking about one piece of it every day. And then homerooms are going to have discussions and send in ideas for our student beliefs. Is that from our ideas, or did the consultant say you should do that?"

"Morris, I remembered what you said a few weeks ago, and I've been looking for a time to do it. The consultant did say that we should get student input, but that's about it—just the general concept. You're giving me the specific ideas about how."

"Cool. Then what's going to happen with the ideas from homerooms?"

"Well, I heard about this Mo and Joe duo, so I thought I'd keep going with a winning team. I'd like to spring you from one of your classes so you can go to Leadership Class with Joe and work with them on summarizing the ideas and decide how to present them to the school improvement team."

"Really? You think my teacher will go along with that?"

"Now, Morris, I may not be a real pushy guy, but I am the principal. I think I can probably make that happen."

Morris grinned from ear to ear as the rest of Table Ten murmured their affirmation. Before the principal turned to move away, he was stopped with one more question.

"Is the school improvement team doing OK on the School Portfolio? I heard one of my teachers say it's really getting out of hand."

Mr. Spark rubbed the back of his neck. "Ouch. I wish that hadn't been said in front of you students, but I have to admit that it seems a little overwhelming. Last time we did accreditation, there wasn't much information to pull together—mainly just dropout rates and the ITED scores—you know, those Iowa Tests of Educational Development. Now there's a lot more test stuff, and we have separate reports for all the different kinds of students—a whole package of pages for each year. I wouldn't say it's out of hand, but I sure couldn't say I've got it under control either."

"Who's allowed to look at it? Is it—like—totally classified or something?"

Mr. Spark chuckled. "I guess we got our points across during testing about security and confidentiality and so forth. The test itself is practically classified, as you say, and information that's attached to any individual student is private. But these reports I'm talking about are the whole school, not specific individuals. It's public information. Any citizen could look at them."

"So . . . since I'm supposed to be practicing responsible citizenship, I'm a citizen of the school and I could look at that stuff."

"You sure *could.* But would you *want* to?"

"Now, Mr. Spark. Don't you say not to judge a person just by their GPA? I'm not getting the best grades in math, but to be honest, I'm so bored I'm just slacking off. I was thinking it would be interesting to help you with that and maybe I could get some extra credit in math. I think my math teacher is on that school improvement team."

"Morris, that's a great idea. If I know Mr. Adams, he'll probably try to work a deal with you—like get serious about his regular expectations *and* do some work for extra credit. I doubt he'll let you off the hook though."

"That's OK. I can do both. It just didn't seem worth the effort before. I'll talk to him."

"Mr. Spark. Hey, Mr. Spark." Morris isn't waiting for the principal to stop by the lunch table at noon. He knows Mr. Spark is always near the main doors, greeting students as they start their day.

"Good morning, Morris. What is that I see? A backpack?"

Morris ducks his head and grins. "Yeah, yeah. I had to break down and use something to carry this megabinder full of data Mr. Adams loaned me. There's a ton of stuff in here—at least it feels like a ton. So many pages of rows and columns of numbers. I've got some ideas about graphing it so it's easier to show interesting stuff. And data analysis is right in my course syllabus, so I can work out a project on this. You know, I never bothered to read a course syllabus before either. But Mr. Adams said I had to show what standards this would connect to. You know, Mr. Spark, it might not be a bad idea if students knew more about these standards. Well, anyway, see you at lunch."

And before Mr. Spark could say, "They're on the Web site," Morris was on his way to unload his burden of data.

As usual at dismissal time (except for district administrator meeting days), Mr. Spark is near the doors as the buses pull up along the patio. He waves to some and calls a few over for personal pep talks, while others seek him out for high fives, handshakes, and even an occasional hug. Morris approaches in his slightly sideways hands-in-pockets shuffle and asks, "Mr. Spark, you think things are going to go OK tomorrow?"

"You mean, sharing the data with the school improvement team? It's going to go just fine. Mr. Adams and I told them that you and Joe would be attending, and Mr. Adams already said you did a great job with your presentation to the class."

"Yeah, I thought I'd better practice, so I put that in my independent study proposal. You know, there's a couple more of us who eat at Table Ten that could do some cool stuff if they could design special projects. They have IEPs—that's 'individual,' right?—but it's all so focused in on their weak areas. If you had to spend your whole time *in* school doing your weak stuff and only used your strengths *out* of school—where would *you* rather be?"

"That's a powerful point, Morris. Another thing for me to ponder. By the way, where's your big binder? That backpack's looking a little skinny."

"Well, Mr. Adams hooked me up with Mr. Ralston in the media center. I don't know if they're supposed to do this or not, but they let me check out a laptop so I could work on my graphs and set up my PowerPoint and everything. Gotta go. See you after school tomorrow."

Mr. Spark didn't tell Morris that some of the teachers on the school improvement team had questioned him about having students come to give a presentation. Nor did he admit that they were the same people who complained that the data weren't user friendly and that they didn't have any time to crunch the numbers themselves. But he did cross his fingers behind his back.

"Hey, Joe. You sure did a good job of talking about the Mission Statement and how your Leadership Class people think students should do some beliefs too. That was great. So you're going to coordinate getting a little survey together so everybody can answer. I'm sure glad you talked first. I've never done anything in front of a bunch of adults before."

"Well, maybe I covered it up OK, but I was kinda nervous myself, Morris. And you did great too. Those stacked bar graphs were awesome. You showed how many kids were at each level in each test for the last five years—all on one page. It really made it obvious that kids are doing better in writing. But the colors for each level showed the bad news too. The red sections that show the amount of kids having a real hard time is hardly changing at all. At first, the teachers were talking about being just as good as the other high schools in the county and a little above the state, and then they switched over to what's getting better and what still needs attention in our own school. You just laid it out so it was right in their faces."

Back in the conference room, the adult members of the school improvement team were chatting in pairs and trios. Some were commenting on the unlikely pairing of "Mo and Joe" as a speaking team. Others were poring over the graphs Morris had created of attendance and discipline and past surveys. He had even graphed the most recent categories of the "sex and violence" survey that Table Ten had criticized.

One pair of teachers was looking at the final version of the revised Mission Statement and commented, "You know, we could organize these graphs by phrases in the Mission Statement. We've got these graphs of test scores that relate to 'mastering essential skills.' And we've got discipline and attendance data that would indicate 'responsible citizenship.' The teen survey might give us some hints about their critical thinking and decision making. We'd just need to get some teacher perceptions about quality of work. That could be baseline data to work from as we improve."

"OK. For the faculty meeting, let's use Morris's PowerPoint slides and put them in order with the Mission categories. There should be enough time to have an activity that will get some comments about high quality work."

QUESTIONS FOR REFLECTION

1. Mr. Spark realized that some teachers might not be enthused to hear students present information about their school. What has he done in the last few months to create readiness? What would be the reaction of teachers in your school?

2. Morris admits that he has not fully applied himself in his math class. Why? What level of effort does your school get from its top students? In light of the No Child Left Behind focus on struggling students, how much attention is being paid to challenging all?

3. Morris and his friends have not been aware of the specific standards they must meet—for class completion, for graduation, for success on the state assessment. Do students in your school know the specific knowledge and skills they must demonstrate? Why? Why not? What important next step may be needed?

4. As you answer these questions in your own thinking, what will you do to check the accuracy of your perceptions with students?

CONTENT FOR CONSIDERATION

Students and Data

Students are both an important source of data for school improvement *and* a resource for the use of data. They can help to organize and display data in creative ways, which is both a service to their school and an authentic learning experience that is directly tied to academic standards and to the world of work. They can help to interpret data by querying it in different ways than adults might and offering a different set of hypotheses and strategies. *Getting Excited About Data: Combining People, Passion, and Proof to Maximize Student Achievement* (Holcomb, 2004) includes suggestions about creating user-friendly data displays and organizing data sets in the school portfolio. Aligning data with the school's core values is demonstrated in an activity called "Monitoring Our Mission" (pp. 62–64).

Service and Service-Learning

The immediate community surrounding the high school student is the school, and working to improve that environment should be considered community service. If graduation requirements include a service requirement, it should not be limited to activities outside the school. One of the recommendations from *Breaking Ranks II* (NASSP, 2004) is that "the high school will promote service programs and student activities as integral to an education, providing opportunities for all students that support and extend academic learning" (p. 125). Benefits listed include findings that participants in student activities have more consistent attendance, better academic achievement, and higher aspirations than nonparticipants. The challenges identified include the difficulty of finding enough activities in which to engage all students, busing, and transportation—and then the challenge of overcoming the perception that service programs must happen outside of school. This paradoxical set of challenges can be ameliorated by engaging students in real problem-solving and improvement activities within their school communities—as an expectation, as a prerequisite to service outside the school, or as an alternative for students particularly challenged by transportation or other logistical factors.

An increasing emphasis in terms of service is to move beyond "hours of volunteering" to actual "service-learning." As described in the *Wisconsin Toolkit for Service-Learning and Citizenship* (Burmaster, 2004), service-learning "has clear and direct ties to academic curriculum in addition to its community outcomes" (p. 5). It isn't field trips, because it can happen within the four walls of the classroom or school. It isn't time away from class, because it *is* class. It is a methodology to achieve core academic outcomes. Service-learning within a school can include tutoring and mentoring, further strengthening the personalization and connections among students and between students and staff.

Service projects that connect with the larger community and the world can emerge from students' own concerns (Burmaster, 2004). Kelsey Swiatko, a junior at Bradford High School in Kenosha, Wisconsin, e-mailed the superintendent of schools:

> In my World Issues Class, we studied Hurricane Katrina and its effects worldwide. A statistic that bothered me was, while as a nation we are very generous, we tend to then forget about our own communities. I wanted to make a difference in my community and not forget about the needs of our shelters.
>
> The shelters get clothes, backpacks, toiletries, etc., but they need NEW UNDERWEAR. So I created and organized "Operation Underwear." With the assistance of the Kenosha WalMart, WISN Channel 12, FM 106.1, 95 WIIL Rock, the *Kenosha News*, friends and family, I am ready to collect those undergarments for distribution to local shelters. My goal is 1,200 pieces in 12 hours.

Kelsey's efforts actually resulted in 2,200 pairs of underwear in only 10 hours. She then entered the 4 Wishes Contest at 95.7 FM WRIT in Milwaukee and was selected as one of four winners. Her family recently drove to Milwaukee to pick up a truckload of various donated items, from toys to underwear. The radio station also provided a link from their Web site to the Web site of Women and Children's Horizons, so Kelsey's gift just keeps on giving.

A STUDENT GETS THE LAST WORD

Nathan Yagi-Stanton is copresident of his junior class at Sammamish High School (Grindeland, 2005). He learned that the school custodian had not seen his family since fleeing Vietnam because he couldn't save enough money to cover the cost of the trip. "We sold T-shirts that read 'Tham 2 Vietnam' and gave him the trip during an assembly. . . . I've found that people want to help and if you tell them the need and give them a way, you can bring those desires together." His current goal is to raise enough money to make the senior prom affordable for every student. "I just get a thrill out of helping people."

December,
Year 1

Morris Minds the C's and R's

"**M**r. Spark, can you believe almost every single student filled out that survey? They were really jazzed about having some beliefs of, by, and for the students. Of course, a lot of the discussions kept coming back to that 'mutually respectful' part of the Mission Statement. So we're thinking of summarizing things around some categories of respect. And we're thinking of what to call them. 'Mission' sounds kind of action oriented. So we don't want to just say we 'believe' certain things. We want to make it like what we promise to do. Got any ideas?"

"Well, Joe, I'll tell you that I'm jazzed too. Teachers are telling me how interested the kids are and how they wish kids would be this engaged in class all the time. So you want to summarize 'promises.' Would that word work?"

"Not quite. Too elementary."

"Hmmm. How about 'pledge'?"

"That's better, but it kinda sounds like a money pledge—or when you sign a pledge. It might work, but . . ."

"What about 'commitment'? Are you making a commitment for mutual respect?"

"Hey, that's better. Commitments. Now we just need something to go with that . . . it'll come to me. Thanks, Mr. Spark. Have a good day."

"Oh, I will," thought Mr. Spark, as Joe headed for class. "I'm having a lot of fun watching all this unfold around me."

"Hi, Morris. How are things going? You look a little down today."

"Well, Mr. Spark, I asked Mr. Adams what happened since I did those graphs and stuff. He said that the school improvement team had to choose some priority areas to work on—so they picked low test scores and discipline policies and grading. That really bums me out. I mean—what if I did all that work and all we end up with is more strict rules and more kids flunking out? How does that make any kind of sense? Maybe I shouldn't have opened up my mouth to you in the first place."

"Oh, Morris. Please don't be discouraged. There are little conversations going on in all the department meetings, and I think before the winter break, I'll be able to describe it to you better. You see, these teachers really do want students to be successful and do quality work—but they have a lot of old models in their minds. So the first thing they're going to think of is what they're used to—rules and grading. I even talked with the consultant about it. He said the most important thing is to keep the conversations going and not shut them down by being too critical right now. I've worked out some questions I'm going to ask at the next school improvement meeting—just to keep them thinking and not settle on any actions too soon. You know, Morris, I really need you to not give up. Be patient and hang in there. You know, when you're young like you, you have a lot to learn. And when you're old like me, you have a lot to *un*learn. And that's even harder."

Morris smiles as the lean and fit Mr. Spark pretends to wobble with a cane. "Okay, then. Just don't let it backfire on us kids, OK?"

"Well, Morris, I've got an update for you. I think you'll be pretty glad we started these discussions after all. Here are the priorities the staff picked to work on—they call them the five R's."

Morris looks at the index card Mr. Spark has laid on the lunch table. "I don't get it—the first line says 'mastery of essential skills'—none of that starts with R."

"Oops, generation gap again, Morris. Back in the day we used to talk about readin', and writin', and 'rithmetic . . ." Morris groans as Mr. Spark lists the three R's by singing the old tune about school and the hickory stick. "The words on the card are from the Mission Statement, but we called them the three R's for fun."

- Mastery of essential skills
- Relationships
- Responsible citizenship

"OK. That makes sense. And I see the other two here do start with *R*—relationships and responsible citizenship. What happened to the talk about discipline and grading?"

"Well, Morris, I asked them some questions about those ideas. And they said we needed to work on those things because students don't show enough respect for them and for each other and don't do their best work. So we did a couple of fishbone diagrams—that's something I learned from the consultant. We did one for 'lack of respect' and one for 'poor quality work.' You put that on the head of the fish and you make a skeleton of the fish by putting all the causes on the bones. By the time we were done, people decided that students—all of us, really—have more respect for people we have some kind of relationship with. So we decided to think about how our structure helps or hinders us from building relationships. And we decided that we want responsibility, not just obedience, from students. Now, don't think there won't be any rules, Morris. I wouldn't want to kid you."

"I know, Mr. Spark. There's always got to be some rules. I'm just relieved to know they aren't the only thing teachers are thinking about. What happens next?"

"When we come back in January, we'll be studying each one of these three priorities some more—getting more specific information, learning what works best from research, and talking about what we do here compared to the best places. So far I'm keeping them from starting on specific plans until we learn more."

The mischief lights go on in Morris's eyes. "Ah, so you have to *un*learn *and* learn. You do need a lot of patience. Thanks for telling me that. The holiday break isn't really all that fun for me, so at least I'm not bummed about the teachers and my data work."

Mr. Spark suddenly realizes things were tough at Morris's house this year with the layoffs at the mill. "Hey, Morris, can you get over to the library branch in your neighborhood? Yeah? Well, let's get that laptop from Mr. Ralston again. Then if you have time, maybe you can get online and do a little research on these topics. But only if you get bored."

"Oh, that's cool. I might find some neat Web sites about high schools or something."

"By the way, Morris, how's Gloria doing? She wasn't at your table the last couple of days."

"Oh, not to worry. I told her about Mr. Adams letting me do up a proposal for extra credit in math, so she started talking to Mrs. Paulson and she's using her free time on some sculpture thing. Did you notice she stopped wearing that black lipstick? Same clothes, but I think she's loosening up a little."

"Hey, Mr. Spark. Got a present for you here." Joe reaches out with a scroll wrapped in red ribbon. "It's those Commitments we've been working on. They've gone from Leadership Class to the whole Student Council, and the reps have shared them in homerooms, so they've been hashed over real good. And we found the other word we were looking for. Miss Pope showed me a real use for a thesaurus. We found a word that starts with a *C* to match 'commitments,' and it means everyone. This is the official copy of our Collective Commitments. See you in the new year."

As Joe hurried away to enjoy the days of holiday freedom, Mr. Spark unrolled the students' declarations.

> **Collective Commitments**
> - Respect others
>   - Take a stand for respectful conduct
>   - Be positive and appropriate in what we say and do
>   - Help people see how their actions impact the rest
>
> - Respect our place
>   - Pick up litter
>   - No graffiti or vandalism
>
> - Respect our chances
>   - Be prepared for class
>   - Use class time well
>   - Work hard
>   - Stretch to be better than we are

"Yes, indeed," he thought. "It does appear a whole new year is unfolding."

QUESTIONS FOR REFLECTION

1. How "mutually respectful" is your school environment? How would you characterize the interactions of staff with each other, of staff with students, and of students with each other? What needs attention?

2. At this point in the change process, the consultant advises patience and the principal makes a commitment to "ask questions" at the next meeting of the school improvement team. Is he being forceful enough? Why? Why not? What would you do?

3. Students are becoming more involved and more candid about situations in their school but still express fear that it might "backfire"

as more punitive discipline. What level of trust is present in your school? How would students react to opportunities for more visible and open input?

4. As the Table Ten Advisory Group becomes more engaged with the principal and the school, Gloria is becoming "less Goth." To what degree do you believe such changes can take place?

5. As you answer these questions in your own thinking, what will you do to check the accuracy of your perceptions with students? Have you found *your* Table Ten yet?

CONTENT FOR CONSIDERATION

Value of Group Process Tools

Students and staff at Knownwell High School participated in the use of an analysis tool that is variously referred to as a fishbone, a cause-and-effect diagram, or an Ishikawa diagram, from its roots in the Deming-prompted quality movement in Japan. This group process tool and others are described in *Asking the Right Questions: Techniques for Collaboration and School Change* (Holcomb, 2001). Such tools can provide valuable assistance to help elicit student voice. It is more comfortable to offer an idea as "something we could put on that diagram" rather than as a more direct input or challenge in an unstructured conversation.

Personalization

One set of recommendations in *Breaking Ranks II* (NASSP, 2004) is identified as the core area of "Personalizing the School Environment" (p. 18). The focus is on "providing students with opportunities to develop a sense of belonging to the school, a sense of ownership over the direction of one's learning, and the ability to recognize one's choices and to make choices based on one's own experience and understanding of the choices." The report specifically recommends that "teachers will convey a sense of caring to their students so that students feel that their teachers share a stake in their learning" and that "the high school community, which cannot be values-neutral, will advocate and model a set of core values essential in a democratic and civil society." The Collective Commitments developed at Knownwell High School represent such a set of core values, and the word *respect* emerges frequently.

The Productive High School (Murphy et al., 2001) also calls for "Building Schools on Humanized, Intellectual Relationships for Learning" (Chapter 8). Three elements of personalization described there include (1) engagement of students in a cohesive, nurturing culture, (2) teachers operating a positive, professionally oriented community, and (3) a community of commitment driven by strong student-adult relationships (p. 160). In their analysis, "students told us 'the way teachers treat you as a student or a person' counted more than any other factor in the school setting in determining their attachment to the school, their commitment to the school's goals, and, by extension, the academic future they imagined for themselves" (McLaughlin, 1994, p. 9).

During the closing general session of ASCD's 2005 Conference on Teaching and Learning, Stephen Sroka (2006) introduced a panel of student experts who answered questions about the kinds of schools they want and the most desirable qualities in teachers. Some highlights of their responses include the following:

- What makes a school a safe and healthy place? Supportive teachers that students can connect with. Teachers who know who you are and can relate to your needs. Being free to speak your mind and being respected.
- What are the qualities of effective teachers? They are nonjudgmental. They let kids know their opinions are welcome and respected. They are outgoing, understanding, and unintimidating, and you can confide in them. They care. They have a passion for the content and the students they teach.

A STUDENT GETS THE LAST WORD

Rick Allen (2004) describes Christopher Unger's interviews of students in three states and includes this poignant example. In a group of African American senior boys on the cusp of failing, Unger asked what they would tell teachers to do that would make a difference if they could start high school over. Despite the teenage posturing and cool reception to the question, one young man finally said, "If teachers cared or at least pretended to care" (p. 5).

January, Year 1

Studying Together

"Happy New Year, Mr. Spark!"

"Welcome back, Morris. How was your break?"

"Well, I didn't get bored. I had that laptop with all that data on it, and I played around some more with it. And when I was online at the library, I went to some Web sites about high schools. You know, there's a lot out there these days about relationships."

"That's true, Morris. I'll tell you what's going to be happening with the school improvement plan now. The school improvement team is going to have study groups going—some about essential skills, some about relationships, and some about responsibility."

"Who's going to be on them?"

"Well, we're challenging every staff member to select one of those topics and be on a study team for the next month or so. I know what you're thinking, and I agree. Why not have some students in there too? Do you think very many students would be interested?"

"I think most everybody would be interested in the topics, but they need more than one way to be involved. Like maybe these topics could be what they do some of their research assignments about, or their persuasive essays, and teachers could bring that to the study groups."

"I don't know why I never thought about our professional development topics being relevant for students too."

"Well, yeah. When we were talking about the Mission Statement, and you said that thing about levels of thinking, I got curious. I still want to know more about that. Besides studying research, what else will these study groups do?"

"They probably will need to do more data analysis as specific questions come up. And they'll be talking about how we do things now—what we call current practices. After all that, they'll be making recommendations for what strategies we should put in place to get better on the five R's."

"Well, if they have them before and after school, there will be kids who want to join. But you'll have to convince them that they will be respected and it will really count. And be sure you don't just take all honor students. They really don't know what school is like for some of my friends."

"Thanks, Morris. That's an excellent reminder."

"And Mr. Spark?"

"Yes, Morris?"

"Can I be in a relationships group? I mean—like I have a relationship with you now and it wasn't rocket science. You just chatted me up now and then. So they don't have to make it all complicated."

"I'm sure they'll be glad to hear that, Morris."

Two days later, Morris was the one glad to hear Mr. Spark on the intercom announcing the formation of study groups and explaining the topics and purpose. He told students they could participate in three ways: just informally writing notes for their teachers to bring or more formally writing up some research or persuasion or actually joining a group. All the teachers had a list of the groups, when they would meet, and the teachers leading the groups so students could communicate their interests directly.

"Way to go, Mr. Spark. You sure started this year out with a bang. And you picked the right teachers to lead the groups. They're pretty much the ones kids like to talk to, so that will be encouraging."

"Thanks, Morris. I'm sure curious to see what happens."

"One thing that's happening is that everybody from my lunch table is going to get involved now. They're starting to believe that at least some of the teachers want to hear from them. Tom and Teri figure they should try one of the study groups about learning essential skills. Miss Pope helped Joe with the name for the Collective Commitments, and Mrs. Donnelly handles their IEPs. I told them it's important that there's ideas from kids who have trouble learning. And Mike's going with Joe on responsibility. He wants to show that skateboarders aren't just irresponsible and can have constructive thoughts about the school too. He thinks Mr. O'Brien's cool. And I'm pretty sure I can get Gloria to go with me to Mrs. Halverson's group about relationships. She's a cool lady. The rest of the counselors pretty much stick to checking your schedule to be sure you have enough credits and stuff. She asks you what's going on in your life."

"And how are things with you, Morris?"

"Well, Dad's still looking for a job, and Mom's trying to get more hours, but we're OK. They're kinda down, and I feel bad about that. But Mom says I seem more serious about school and that makes her feel better. So now, between you and my mom, you've got me hooked."

"You hang in there, Morris. I hope you realize that you're making a big difference here, and I'm sure that helps with your feelings when you're home too."

"Yep, if there's at least one or two bright spots in a day, we can keep on going. Some kids don't even have that."

As Mr. Spark moved on to check some suspicious activity down the hall, he wondered if Morris's friends would open up in the study groups— and if those he was approaching had their fair share of bright spots.

"OK. Time for updates here." Morris focused the random chatter of the emerging leaders at Table Ten. "I checked with Mr. Spark about what should be happening in our study groups. There's three things for this stage. We're supposed to dig deeper into that data in the School Portfolio and find more details about our areas—essential skills, relationships, or responsibility. Like what specific skills should be the focus. And we're supposed to research the best ways that other schools are working on those things and what experts think high schools should be doing. The third is that we should have honest discussions about what happens here in our school and how it's the same or different from what we research. So, does that sound like what you heard in the first group meeting?"

Tom and Teri looked at each other. Tom shrugged. Teri spoke. "Mrs. Donnelly said just about that exact same thing. And Miss Pope said one you left out. She said everything should match up with the Mission and the Collective Commitments. So like in our group, we'd be carrying out the parts on 'diverse and challenging learning experiences' and 'practicing critical thinking.'"

"That's right, Morris. Mrs. Halverson said that our focus on relationships is connected to the 'mutually respectful' environment and our statements about respect for others, our place, and our chances."

"Oh, yeah. Thanks, Gloria. I was tracking on what Mr. Spark said, and I'm glad you're tuning in on Mrs. Halverson. Between the two of us, we'll get it right. Mike, is your group with Joe and Mr. O'Brien starting off good?"

"Hmm. I guess. They said we'd look at discipline data some more. I hope it's not going to be aimed at how bad us skateboarders are. And we talked about 'producing high quality work' and 'practicing responsible citizenship.' I'm not sure about research. I might have tuned out a little when I heard about discipline."

"Not to worry, Mike. Be sure you don't take things too personally. Now, one suggestion. I talked Mr. Spark's secretary out of five file folders, and I think we should keep notes and stuff from our groups in here. We won't see each other every day because some of the groups are at lunchtime, but let's make sure on Fridays we get together without fail."

QUESTIONS FOR REFLECTION

1. At Knownwell High School, students will be studying the same topics that teachers study and may even participate in their discussion groups. What would be the reaction at your school? Are there topics about schools and teaching that should only be accessible to adults? Why? Why not?

2. Morris gives Mr. Spark the reminder "Don't just take all honor students." Which students are involved in your school? Are specific efforts made to engage the struggling learners and the marginal behavers?

3. Among the staff in your school, who are "the ones kids like to talk to"? What are the indicators that you used to identify them?

4. As you answer these questions in your own thinking, what will you do to check the accuracy of your perceptions with students?

CONTENT FOR CONSIDERATION

Advisories and Extracurriculars

In *The Productive High School* (Murphy et al., 2001), a section on student-adult relationships begins with this powerful quote from Ogden and Germinario (1995):

A primary indicator of a student's sense of belonging in a school is the quality of interactions and relationships he/she has with the adults in that school . . . who help model the world for the child . . . on whom the child relies for security, support, and recognition. Through the development of trust between students and those adults around them, fear and apprehension are managed. . . . [S]tudents are far more likely to take intellectual risks in classrooms, to feel free to engage in activities throughout the school and to seek adult assistance when confronted with a school or life problem. (p. 78)

One antidote that is recommended is a teacher advisory program, in which a teacher meets regularly with and advises a small group of students. These arrangements are credited by one researcher as "the best way I know of to ensure that no more of our teenagers slip through the cracks of the system and are lost to us" (Tye, cited in Murphy, 2001, p. 187). Other writers describe advisory groups as places where students "learn communication skills, conflict management, decision-making skills, and other important life skills in a setting that is comfortable and safe, and an adult they know and trust guides them" (Murphy, 2001, p. 188). Additional information and resources for advisories can be found in *Changing Systems to Personalize Learning: The Power of Advisories* (Osofsky, Sinner, & Wolk, 2003) and *Student Advisories in Grades 5–12: A Facilitator's Guide* (MacLaury, 2002).

In some high school settings where teachers do not get to know their students in the classroom or advisories, the only structure that helps develop teacher-student interactions may be the range of extracurricular activities provided. Participation in school activities helps participants develop common ground and build social ties. Shared activities bind students and teachers to each other and the institution, increasing connection, commitment, and engagement in the work of the school. These realities prompted student leader Scott Frost (see the Epilogue) to focus his efforts on an Activities Fair and a goal of every student becoming involved in at least one school activity.

The Unheard Voice of the "Middle" Student

Even in suburban schools like Naperville North High School, issues of connectedness surface (Grier, 2000). Administrators there noted that "top performers have long received lots of attention. The many problems of those at the bottom are at least addressed by everything from church groups to federal government grants. But it is the ones who just float through their four years, not flunking, doing nothing special, who might benefit from a little added effort."

In "Psychological Bars to School Improvement," Douglas Heath (2000) describes the dangers of not listening to and respecting students. He cautions that "aging adults are at risk of losing touch with the changing inner worlds of their students. Today's students' minds are more vulnerable to distraction and so to boredom, relationships more hurtful, values more uncertain, and self-confidence and self-command more fragile. Teachers often are not aware of these vulnerabilities."

A STUDENT GETS THE LAST WORD

A contrasting article reports about schools who do listen (Easton, 2002). Philip is a student who wrote about "an awesome teacher" who would listen to feedback and act on it. "That teacher's class," he said, "taught me that it is OK to give the teacher suggestions about what can be done to make the class better."

February, Year 1

Mr. Shepley's Epiphany

"**H**ey, everybody. How've you been? What's shakin' in your worlds the last week or so?"

"Morris, you wouldn't believe all the data we've been talking about. And me, Teri, the terrible student, sitting there saying stuff like 'mean' and 'mode' and if the difference is significant or not and why we need to have longitudinal trend data instead of this one-year stuff. It's the first time I've ever had a real-life use for those terms Mrs. Donnelly drilled into me. If you didn't know that stuff, you could jump to way wrong conclusions, and this school improvement stuff would never work."

"Well, you wouldn't believe what wrong conclusions *do* get made—by the teachers even! Mr. Shepley is in the Relationships group with Morris and me. He admitted that he signed up for that one because it's the only one he could handle in his schedule. All he wants to do is argue against the data. Like he says, 'This teen survey is just self-report stuff. They could just be making it all up.'" Gloria's uncanny switch to a gruff male voice caused momentary laughter at the lunch table, and then dead silence as she continued in her own voice. "He doesn't believe how many kids think about suicide. He says it's just exaggerating to get attention."

Mike chimed in. "Well, duh. Thinking about suicide—or trying it anyway—that *is* the ultimate attention-getter. Hasn't he heard of 'a cry for help'?"

"I don't think he's really tuned in to any of that. He just loves science, you know. He's really into his experiments. When we talked about how almost a third of the students said they don't have an adult in the school to be confidential with, he said, 'That's not my job. That's what counselors are for.' I wanted to scream. There's four counselors and 1,200 kids. But Mrs. Halverson is so mellow. She didn't even act mad because he was laying it on the counselors. She just used that soothing voice of hers and said, 'Do you suppose there could be a connection between that attitude and kids getting desperate enough for attention to think of suicide?'"

"Oooh. That's ba-ad. Didn't know Mrs. Halverson had it in her."

"Anyway, he's really outnumbered, thank goodness. Everybody else in the group is really concerned about students having good connections in the school. They shot him down too when he was complaining about school improvement." Gloria's voice changed again. "'Our test scores are just as good as every other high school in the county and even a little above the state average. What's wrong with that?!' And that's when Mr. Benton said, 'What's wrong with it is that we have above-average kids and teachers. Like you—I assume you'd agree—you've been state Teacher of the Year in science.' Then Mr. Shepley says, 'True. True.' And shuts up for the rest of the time. But I have to admit. He did agree to do the same as everybody else in the group and talk to six kids individually to clarify some questions about that survey data. It's got to be two A students, two C students, and two D/F list students. It won't be hard for him to get the full range, 'cause he's such a grade-on-the-curve guy. Funny—he thinks it's going to disturb his whole unit plan to talk to a couple of kids each day, but I think he was so outnumbered he had to say he would do it."

"We talked about the survey in Responsibility group too," reported Joe. "There's a couple of teachers who act like it's all on us kids—that we're just not motivated and won't take responsibility. But Mr. Soderberg started telling them how we have jobs and how some of us help at the homeless shelter and tutor kids at the elementary down the street and collected toys for needy families back at Christmastime. And then one of them walked right into it and said, 'So why don't they take responsibility for their learning then?' And then Mike—yeah, Mike, the tough, silent guy—just couldn't back down. He said, 'Why don't you guys give us any responsibility for our learning? You tell us every single thing—what to do, when, where, how, and it's all your way or the highway. I mean, we're like puppets you want to manipulate. Does a puppet take responsibility?' Then Mike turned beet red in the face and looked really shocked at himself, but several teachers said, 'That's OK, Mike, it's time we heard from you.'"

Nonverbal affirmations of Mike's message spun around the circle at Table Ten, and Tom asked, "So, Mike, did they zap you with the discipline data like you thought they would?"

"Not really. It's too general right now. We need some kind of breakdown about kinds of incidents and groups of kids and times of the day and areas in the school before we can go further with this. And I'm ready to face it—there will be some incidents of skateboard damage on the patio. It's not me, but I don't have any way to stop some other guys."

"That was kind of true in Relationships group too—how general the data is in the School Portfolio. Now I know why Mr. Spark said we would have to 'dig deeper' into it. But respect came up again. Teachers said the biggest reason they kick kids out of class is for lack of respect. So we asked them what they meant, and they said stuff like rolling our eyes or saying 'whatever.' We tried to explain that's just us being teenagers. That they shouldn't overreact and take it so personal. I mean—if somebody moves their eyes, but at the same time they are really doing what you want them to, we think that's still respect."

"Well, Miss Pope and Mrs. Donnelly already did more with the discipline stuff than your groups. I'll tell them they need to share their work—Ha! They went from the graphs back to the original sources—the pink slips from last year. And they sorted them a bunch of different ways. One thing they noticed is a lot of ninth graders getting in trouble right away in the first few months. And kids getting kicked out of English and social studies more than other classes."

"That ninth-grade stuff isn't rocket science. You go from middle school, having four main teachers who are on the same team, working together—to seven periods a day, with all different teachers dictating their own separate rules to their students. I remember one teacher who gave out a one-page course syllabus and a two-page list of rules and consequences. Seems he cared more about keeping us in line than learning anything. He's retired now, though—good thing."

"Yeah, by the time you get to the end of the first day and every teacher has reviewed their rules, you feel like you're in prison or something."

"Easy now," Morris cautions the group. "Let's not get too worked up on just one thing. We just got the Collective Commitments and there's some simple bullet points under them that could just be the whole-school rules. Joe and I will talk some more about that. Now, what did you say about English and social studies?"

"Well, Miss Pope is the English Department head, and she already interviewed the teachers to see when kids act out. And she matched up the kids who are getting kicked out of class with their middle school test scores. She had read this stuff about fake reading and reading aversion and thinks that when everybody's going to have to read out loud, they might be getting kicked out on purpose, because it's less embarrassing than not being able to read."

"Sounds like me," Tom grins. "You have to read a lot in social studies too. But we have tough reading in science. What makes science different?"

"Well, Mrs. Donnelly said kids have a chance to use more modalities in science and art and PE and tech ed and so on. Like—not just sit and take notes and read, but do hands-on stuff. So maybe kids don't get as frustrated or don't want to be out of class and miss out on the fun stuff like experiments and projects."

"That makes some sense. I never heard of modalities, but it sounds like special education."

"You're right. It's in my IEP that I learn best through kinesthetic modality—doing stuff. But my teachers don't seem to get that. And anyways, I think *all* teachers should do a variety of stuff for all kids. If they'd let us, or ask us, we could tell them the way we learn best. We've had about 10 years already of trying to learn, so we have some idea even if we don't know the teacher lingo."

"Right on, Teri. We know they can't teach 27 different ways every hour, but they could give us some choices or let us make proposals like I did with Mr. Adams."

"Mike, you should be feeling a whole lot better about discipline data if it gets us to sensible rules and more variety in classes."

"Right. But I also want to hear about kids who have trouble reading."

"We're going to talk about that some more next time in the Three R's group. There's a way we can look at the reading tests and check out how many kids had trouble with different things on it. I have a feeling that 'reading' will be the R we talk about the most."

"Well, here we are again. Everybody doing OK? Great hair, Gloria. Lookin' good. Be sure you tell everybody about Mr. Shepley. And anything more on discipline data, Mike? And what about the Three R's?"

"Slow down, Morris. You're really wired today. What's up?"

"Just relieved more than wired, guys. My dad's finally getting some job interviews, so we're thinking things will ease up some at home. Anyways, how are these groups going?"

"You told Gloria to tell us about Mr. Shepley. So give her a chance. What's up?"

"It's nothing much, maybe. But he came back and said he really did talk to six kids. I mean, that is one thing about him—if he says he'll do something, he'll stick to his word even if he's not excited about it. But anyway, he just said that he was glad he did it because he was really shocked. He thought a D/F kid might say he was depressed about school because he couldn't keep up. But one of the A students he talked to also said she gets very depressed because she's afraid of not measuring up to all the hype she hears from her parents and teachers about getting into the best college and going to medical school and how she must fully utilize all her potential, and on and on. He never realized that good students are normal kids too and get bummed out. He said he asked her why she never told anybody she felt so much pressure, and she said nobody ever asked. He said he felt pretty guilty. He even said it was actually pretty interesting to talk to a couple of kids each day for a few minutes. He liked it when he figured out he could do it while we're working or when we're just milling around getting started."

"Wow. Gloria, how can you say that's 'nothing much'? That's like a quantum leap in just a week or two. WOW! There might be hope for some of these dinosaurs after all. Oops, sorry, Morris—gotta show respect. And it was pretty gutsy of him to be so honest."

"That's true, and thanks for the self-correction there, Tom. Who else has an update?"

"Well, in Responsibility, we're talking about kids who like certain activities that aren't in the school day, like skateboarding and chess and some other stuff. I'd have never thought that the smart kids would get in trouble for skipping class too—guess they hide out in the back of the library and keep playing chess instead of going to class. We told them if we had a way to sort of be an official group, we could probably take responsibility for some of the problems we create. So we're looking at how Leadership Class is set up here, compared to other places. You can't really change the Student Council structure, because that's like national, but we can recommend some other ways to be organized. So stay tuned on that one. And I told some of my buddies to cool it on the patio and give it a rest. We don't want to ruin our chances."

"Cool. Good work, Mike. That's even one of the Collective Commitments—respect our chances."

"And what's going on in Three R's? Mike wanted to know more about reading in particular."

"Well, we looked at what you have to do in order to pass that state test. And it doesn't matter if it's the reading test or the math test or the science or social studies test. If you can't read the passages, and read the directions of what to do, you are dead in the water. But it's different reading. We do pretty good when we're just reading stuff from stories and figuring out the main character or the climax in the plot and all that. We've been doing that since elementary. But we really suck in the category they call 'analyzing informational text.' And nobody really taught us that. I mean, we came to high school and got these 3-inch-thick textbooks and pages to read every night—but it's a way different kind of reading. And the questions on these state tests aren't stuff you can just memorize like states and capitals and wars and dates and presidents in order. You have to draw conclusions. So, I was right, we're going to zero in on the R of reading—but not just as a reading class. We're going to study up some more about how to read math stuff, and science and social studies stuff."

"That sounds good, but it's kind of narrow, don't you think? I mean, it would help with our reading assignments, but what about the time we're in the class periods?"

"Well, we actually decided that if so many kids think school is boring, we should find out what they wish class time would be like. So we're going to use a short survey and get more information from kids. Meanwhile, the teachers are going to be looking at their books and journals so we can study what works best. Sure would be nice if there's some stuff kids want that matches up with some stuff teachers find in research."

"Right on! That would make it a lot easier to agree on things to do for that school improvement plan."

QUESTIONS FOR REFLECTION

1. Secondary teachers are certified with a subject matter focus and are sometimes accused of loving their content more than loving their students. To what degree would that be true in your school? Why? Why not?

2. How is perceptual data (surveys, focus groups, etc.) gathered in your school? In what areas do teacher and student perceptions show the most agreement? The most discrepancy?

3. Students and staff at Knownwell High School are becoming very specific in their use of data, for example, drilling into the academic data on reading and subdividing the discipline data on ninth graders. What practices for data analysis are in use in your school?

4. As you answer these questions in your own thinking, what will you do to check the accuracy of your perceptions with students?

CONTENT FOR CONSIDERATION

School Stress and School Connectedness

Mr. Shepley is probably not alone in being unaware of the stress experienced by students. According to the American Federation for Suicide Prevention, suicide is the third leading cause of death among high school and college students. In some studies, 20 percent of adolescents have said they've thought about suicide at one time or another (Franklin, 2005). It is extremely difficult to predict suicide, but one of the indicators is changes in behavior—normally attentive and meticulous students turning in sloppy and unfinished work, normally well-groomed children becoming unkempt and drastically changing hair and clothing styles. If "schools do not ensure that every student feels close to at least one supportive adult at school" (Blum, 2005), who will be aware of such changes and inquire about what is happening with the student?

In the most basic sense, "the act of learning is a very human endeavor—one that is undermined if students are distracted by bullies, teachers fail to challenge students, or struggling students are ignored and forgotten"

(Stover, 2005, p. 31). According to Brian Perkins (cited in Stover, 2005), who surveyed 33,000 urban students, "[I]t is important whether students feel safe, believe adults care about them, and develop values of respect and citizenship. In our urban districts where students are exposed to drive-by shootings, drug overdoses, and domestic violence, students expressed the expectation that they would not live past the age of 25." In another school, he found that 70 percent of students reported a lack of respect for teachers, and 90 percent of teachers reported they didn't feel as though they were respected (pp. 31–32). Principals and staff in this school conducted focus groups with students, added teacher training, brought in speakers to talk to students, and established a conflict mediation program. Over time, there has been improvement in student attitudes about teachers, suspensions have declined, daily attendance increased, and more students in class has meant more time spent learning.

School stress is not just a factor of life for struggling and urban students. Recent research presents the troubling view that high-achieving students feel driven by the expectation to "do everything and do it well" (Pope & Simon, 2005). They feel compelled to compromise their values and manipulate the system and admit to scheming, lying, and cheating to get the grades they believe they need for future success. These college-bound students are often overwhelmed with school, home, and work responsibilities, on top of the usual adolescent passages of puberty and changing relationships with parents. As one student says, "I sometimes have two or three days where I only get two hours of sleep per night. I see lots of my friends burned out, but I don't have time to worry about this. . . . Some people see health and happiness as more important than grades and college; I don't. I feel compelled to compete because we have a really smart class, and I am competing with them to get into college" (Pope & Simon, 2005, p. 34).

School stress affects all students, and Klem and Connell (2004) note that "by high school, as many as 40 to 60 percent of all students—urban, suburban and rural—are chronically disengaged from school" (p. 262). School connectedness is an "important factor in reducing the likelihood that adolescents will engage in health-compromising behaviors and also increases the likelihood of academic success" (Blum, 2005, p. 17). Students who feel connected to school (regardless of their academic success) are less likely to use substances, exhibit emotional distress, demonstrate violent or deviant behavior, experience suicidal thoughts or attempt suicide, or become pregnant. They are less likely to skip school or be involved in fighting, bullying, and vandalism (Blum, 2005, p. 17). Among the strategies Blum recommends for increasing school connectedness are avoiding tracking; setting high academic standards; limiting school size; forming multidisciplinary education teams; ensuring that every student has an adviser; providing mentorship programs; ensuring relevancy in course content; providing service opportunities; providing experiential, hands-on learning activities; using a wide variety of instructional methods, such as extending the class period, school day, or year; and providing opportunities for students who are falling behind to catch up.

The Reading Challenge

One of the main reasons students fall behind in the first place is the challenge of independent reading required in their classes. "People who read well often take for granted the real-world payoffs. Struggling readers seldom get to experience how great it feels to finish a book. Or how helpful it is to read and understand a chapter in a textbook. They don't know how much fun it can be to escape day-to-day life by jumping into a good read. By ninth grade, many students have been defeated by test scores, letter grades, and special groupings. Struggling readers are embarrassed by their labels and often perceive reading as drudgery. They avoid it at all costs" (Tovani, 2000, p. 9).

A STUDENT GETS THE LAST WORD

In "No Choice but Success" (2005), Corbett, Wilson, and Williams talk about the need for schools to remove failure as an option. They describe teachers who simply will not accept excuses, and couple that relentless expectation with support for learning. One of the students describes this tenacity:

> In English class, the teacher is like what I want to have in all my classes. We've had things in there I'm not used to doing. But she say [sic] to me, "You are too intelligent to stop doing what you are working on; you are a good person; you have the knowledge to do the work." If I don't understand it, she will sit down and explain it to me. . . . If something is really hard, she will stay after school to help. . . . I like the teacher to pay attention to what I'm doing. (p. 11)

10

March, Year 1

Students Define Learning

"**O**K, folks. Last time we got together, Teri was telling us about how the Three R's group was thinking of a short survey to see what students wish classes would be like. In the meantime, my group—Relationships—was talking about getting kids' ideas about respect. Now I'm getting worried these study groups are going to drive us nuts with a whole bunch of little surveys. I mean, first they don't seem to listen to us at all, and now everybody wants to survey us."

"Hey, Morris, don't be a sucker. Maybe they just want to do surveys because they don't want to deal with the data they already have."

"Ooh, that's cold, Mike. Give them a little respect too. We want to be given the benefit of the doubt, so let's do the same for the teachers."

"Yeah, and above all, remember, it's Mr. Spark we trust. It might not look like it, but he keeps a pretty close eye on what's going on. He heard about surveys coming out from more than one study group, so he came into ours and asked us to design it so it would include the respect question and just be one survey. Then Mr. O'Brien asked Miss Pope to put a question on the survey about quality work. We talked about keeping it simple, and we talked about how to make sure that people get to say what they want. So we ruled out multiple-choice items and decided to just have some short, open-ended questions."

"That sounds good. I always end up having trouble picking just one answer. So what did you come up with?"

"We-e-ell . . . now that you finally get down to business and ask me . . . I just happen to have a draft of it right here. Because Mr. Spark wants our reaction. There's some more little groups like our table bubbling up around the school, and he's just bouncing ideas off us informally. What do you think of this?"

"Wow. That information at the top is just what we talked about. That they should realize not everybody has the same ideas as the A students."

"Yeah. And sometimes it's easier for girls, so maybe they'll sort that out."

"I like it because it's not full of fancy teacher lingo and you don't have to write a lot. I counted, and there's only 10 letter spaces and you don't even have to use them all because it says 'up to three.'"

"And it's good that it's just one page. That might keep some people from just going off and rambling on and on."

"But some kids are going to take cheap shots anyway."

"Yeah. The teachers said they know they'll get some garbage that might make them mad and some inappropriate answers that might upset them or make them sad. But they said they can toughen up for it, and they do want to know what we're thinking."

"Well—this is great. When are we going to do it?"

"Mr. Spark is going to tell us during the announcements. He's going to ask people to be thinking about respect and effort and what makes a good class. And then tomorrow he'll come on the intercom during one of our classes and say that everybody is going to take class time to fill it out right then. He said that thinking about your learning and effort *is* the kind of critical thinking that should happen in classes, so he's not worried if we take part of the class period. And here's what he told teachers—to have a student collect them and bring them to the office so they will really be anonymous. And he said to tell kids we won't count off for wrong spelling and stuff. It just has to be legible. But we'll throw it away if there's swearing in it."

"Say what?! He said *we* won't count off . . . and *we* would throw it away. He means the teachers, right? Who's going to read these? The one problem with no multiple choices is that it won't be easy to add up the answers."

"Well, there's going to be three different ways of analyzing them. First they'll separate them into piles by boys or girls and another set of piles by the grades they put. Then at the faculty meeting next week, they're going to be in the computer lab with the desktops and also everybody's laptop, and each teacher is going to have 10 of these and they're going to enter the main phrases from the responses. Then they're going to just give their impressions of the most frequent answers, and Mr. Spark is going to write them on the overhead for people to start thinking about. The more scientific approach is going to be done by one of the teachers who's working on her master's degree, and she wants this data for her thesis. So she's going to use some software to do more thematic analysis, just to verify this."

"That makes sense. What's the third way?"

"Mr. Spark is going to make an extra copy of all the surveys and let student volunteers come into the media center before or after school or at

Figure 10.1   Student Survey About Classes, Respect, and Effort

We are gathering information to help us plan for improvements in our school. We truly want honest answers, and at least one staff member will read every single response. We also know that different people have different experiences at school, so please give us this information but not your name. Please check the most appropriate answer:

Male _____ Female _____   Mainly my grades are: A _____ B_____ C_____ D _____ F_____

I generally give   ____ my best effort on everything   ____ some effort on everything
                    ____ best effort but only on things I like   ____ as little effort just to get by

Please answer the following:

1. Some students are saying that their classes are boring. If you agree, please list up to three things that make them boring.

    a.

    b.

    c.

2. We hear that students want respect. If you agree, please tell us one thing that makes you feel you are not respected and one thing that would make you feel more respected.

    a.

    b.

3. We think students are capable of higher quality work than we see in assignments. Please tell us one or two things that would make you want to do your very best work.

    a.

    b.

4. Think of one class that you find interesting and where you do your best work. Please tell us three things about that class that you wish were true in other classes.

    a.

    b.

    c.

lunch—or from class if their work is caught up—and read through them ourselves. They'll be in packets of 10, and the main themes the teachers found will be on the board. Each student will put a check by the themes they agree are in the surveys they read—and if they think there was a main idea the teachers missed, Mr. Ralston will add it to the charts."

"What if there's not enough students to read them all?"

"Well, Mr. Spark said if even half of them get read, it will be a good representation, especially since we have them in categories and Mr. Ralston will give out the packets so an equal number from each category gets included. And the data analysis by the teachers will include every single one. Our reading is a double check to be sure they're getting it right."

"That's pretty cool. This sort of goes with the data project I did with Mr. Adams. Maybe I can talk to him about making some graphs from the results."

"Okay, folks. Did everybody read some of those student surveys? And get your other friends to do it too?"

"C'mon, Morris, you know we did. It was pretty fascinating. Not rocket science at all—we could have predicted the results, but yet this proves it's not just a few of us trying to be heard."

"Right. Everybody talks about respect. Of course, there's different versions of that. Like, some people want to call teachers by their first names, and that might be OK in some places, but not in this town. It's pretty conservative here."

"That's OK with me. I'm more with the idea of showing respect by knowing *our* names. And asking us to do things rather than just 'commanding' us. Even though we know we don't have a choice, it's just a different feeling to be told the expectations and have reasons for them—instead of just like a threat if you don't do it."

"The answers about doing quality work were pretty interesting. Some people said they wanted more choices in how to do stuff, and some said they needed more help, but the most comments were about the *teacher*, not the work."

"That's right. We'll bust our you-know-whats for teachers who care about us and act like we're really important and can do good things. Sort of like an army movie where they say 'this officer's so good I'd follow him anywhere.'"

"The first and last questions were about classes and teaching. And they almost matched up with each other. Like classes are boring because there's too much lecture, and good classes have a variety of activities."

"There's a match in doing our best also. Kids say they give up if they can't get help when they're stuck, and they also say that in good classes there are ways to get help."

"So—getting help is really important. If kids keep saying they want help, that must mean they *want* to do good work, so that doesn't sound like *un*motivated students, does it? Was that mostly the students who checked lower grades at the top?"

"Yes, but there really weren't that many differences between what various groups said. The main one between boys and girls is boys want more hands-on projects and girls want more discussions."

"Blah-blah-blah-blah-blah. No mystery in that," says Mike, grinning at Gloria. She responds with a quick "Watch your mouth!" A chorus of voices join in warning, "Gloria's coming out of her shell, so you better beware."

"All right. Pretty similar answers from boys and girls. What kind of differences by their grades?"

"There is one mystery there. The obvious part is that the kids with lower grades are the ones saying that there should be help available and that good teachers show respect by acting like they believe you can do it. And they said in good classes there are charts and things on the wall that help you stay focused and remember where you are from the last time. Whereas some of the A and B students say they want more challenge and more up-to-date topics."

"So, what's the mystery?"

"Well, some of the A and B kids say just save them time and tell them what to do and what's on the test so they can memorize it and get it over with."

"Whew. That doesn't sound like respecting your chances or doing best quality work. I wonder where that's coming from?"

"Guess we'll have to ask Joe what he thinks about that, since he's the only straight-A guy that hangs out with us sometimes."

"OK, it'll be 'Mo and Joe' again to figure that one out. Meanwhile, here's my notes about what we know so far. I figured I'd better keep some stuff in this folder Morris pillaged from the office."

"So—students have pretty common ideas about what good classes would be like and what would get them to do their best quality work. And several things really matched up with each other. I sure hope something matches up with what teachers are studying from their books and journals and going to conferences."

QUESTIONS FOR REFLECTION

1. Both staff and students had trust issues with regard to the student survey. What were they and how were they addressed? Would they be present in your school?

2. Figure 10.2 shows the responses at Knownwell High School. If this survey was given in your school, what would students identify as their concerns?

3. To what degree do students in your school put forth their best effort and do their best quality of work? Why? Why not?

4. As you answer these questions in your own thinking, what will you do to check the accuracy of your perceptions with students?

Figure 10.2   Student Concerns and Recommendations

STUDENT CONCERNS	SURVEY SAYS . . .

Boring classes—
     too much lecture
     teacher even acts bored
     already know all the stuff
     too hard and there's no help so
         tune out
	Have a variety of activities
	 Show enthusiasm about what they teach
	 Tell us what we'll learn and why it's important
	 Get us into discussions and projects
	 Let us work in groups sometimes
	 Show us examples and demonstrate what they
	     want us to do
	 Check if we understand before giving
	     assignment or going on to next thing
	 Get us thinking
	 Put up charts and give us outline forms and
	     stuff to get organized
	 Have a way to get help in class and later

Lack of respect from teachers—
     put you down when you have ideas
     act like they think you won't get it anyway
	Ask our ideas and input and use them
	 Know our names and something about us
	 Give expectations with reasons, not just
	     threats

Don't do my best because it's not relevant
 Can't do my best because there's no help
     when I need it
	Do my best when teacher cares about me and
	     shows belief in me
	 Teacher gives some options so I feel like it's
	     my best work
	 There's a good reason I should be able to
	     know or do what they are demanding
	 I can get help when I'm stuck so I can keep
	     going

TEACHER CONCERNS	**STUDY SAYS . . .**
Low test scores	
Poor quality work	
Lack of student motivation	
Lack of respect from students	

CONTENT FOR CONSIDERATION

Dropout Factors

Students make decisions about their value in school based on aspects of relationships and connectedness explored in previous sections. Students also make decisions about how heavily to invest in doing quality work and learning to high levels of thought and understanding. Washington State's report on *Helping Students Finish School* (Bergson, 2004) points out that "[e]ducation institutions themselves contribute significantly to the dropout problem. Discipline and grading policies, school organization and size, program assignments, course content, the type of instruction, school climate, and adult-student relationships can all influence students to drop out" (p. 38). The report also lists school-related factors identified by the National Dropout Prevention Center as conflict between home and school culture, ineffective discipline system, lack of adequate counseling, negative school climate, lack of relevant curriculum, passive instructional strategies, inappropriate use of technology, disregard of student learning styles, retentions/suspensions, low expectations, and lack of language instruction (pp. 38–39).

Instruction—Powerful and Differentiated

There is a close connection between some of these factors that impact negatively and strategies that have been found to be powerful in engaging student learning and contributing to high achievement. For example, passive instructional strategies and disregard of learning styles is the negative version of Marzano's findings about "classroom instruction that works" (Marzano, Pickering, & Pollock, 2001). Based on a meta-analysis of studies that report impact on learning, "the essential nine" were identified as

- Identifying similarities and differences
- Summarizing and note taking
- Reinforcing effort and providing recognition
- Homework and practice
- Nonlinguistic representations
- Cooperative learning
- Setting objectives and providing feedback
- Generating and testing hypotheses
- Cues, questions, and advance organizers

Consistent use of this range of strategies would address the challenge of "Adapting to differences—Ensure teachers use a variety of instructional strategies and assessment to accommodate individual learning styles" (NASSP, 2004, p. 6). Although seen more frequently in professional development and practice in elementary schools, differentiated instruction is critical at the secondary level to meet the range of experiences and styles that is even more pronounced by adolescence.

In an online resource (ASCD, n.d.), the Association for Supervision and Curriculum Development provides descriptors of a differentiated secondary classroom, including the following:

- Teachers and students accept and respect one another's similarities and differences.
- Assessment is an ongoing diagnostic activity that guides instruction. Learning tasks are planned and adjusted based on assessment data.
- All students participate in respectful work—work that is challenging, meaningful, interesting, and engaging.
- The teacher is primarily a coordinator of time, space, and activities rather than a provider of information. The aim is to help students become self-reliant learners.
- Students and teachers collaborate in setting class and individual goals.
- Students work in a variety of group configurations, as well as independently. Flexible grouping is evident.
- Time is used flexibly in the sense that pacing is varied, based on student needs.
- Students often have choices about topics they wish to study, ways they want to work, and how they want to demonstrate their learning.
- The teacher uses a variety of instructional strategies to help target instruction to student needs.
- Students are assessed in multiple ways, and each student's progress is measured at least in part from where that student begins.

Perceptions from students are particularly helpful when deliberate attempts are made to include the voices of struggling students. Often the students who are engaged are those who have been successful with traditional teaching practices. As Shirley Hord (cited in Easton, 2004) points out, "Students can be a critical source of information about practices that need to be improved. By using student interviews or student-led focus groups, teachers, parents, administrators, and other stakeholders can validate or disprove what they may see as teachers' best practices. After all, is it the practice itself—or how it affects student achievement—that allows us to list it among our best practices?" (p. 51).

Angela Vaughan is a high school math teacher who has figured out how to let students—freshmen in particular—take more control of their learning (Vaughan, 2005). She designed her course by establishing "overarching expectations and objectives but gave students a large role in deciding how best to achieve those objectives. Students would reflect on the following questions and decide for themselves how they might best learn the material: What resources are available, and which ones should I use to learn this information? How much information do I already know about this topic, and where are the gaps in my understanding? How much and what type of practice should I engage in? When should I complete this work? Do I want to work alone, or would it be more helpful to work with a classmate? When should I take an exam?" (p. 70). A typical day in her class includes 10 minutes of warm-up, 10–15 minutes of presentation, and

60 minutes of student planned activities, followed up by 5–10 minutes checking students' planning sheets. She noted that students assigned themselves more homework, took exams on Mondays, paid attention to lectures, rarely disrupted class, came in for extra help, and 95 percent passed 12 exams over the course of the year, when previous classes had passed none.

Gender Differences and Reading

This variation of teaching approaches may be particularly critical for male students. The Southern Regional Education Board surveyed 40,000 male and female students ("Boys' Academic Slide," 2003) and found striking differences. For example, 70 percent of the girls thought it was useful to do well in school to achieve life goals, while only 57 percent of the boys felt the same. Among potential causes were that schools let boys off the hook in reading, that parents don't stress the importance of boys' education, that schools don't ensure that boys graduate, and that society writes off "average" students who are neither advanced nor identified for special education. The article refers to 12th-grade NAEP scores, on which 44 percent of girls ranked proficient in reading, compared to 28 percent of boys.

The difference in attitudes may certainly be related to differences in school success, and these differences may actually be related to brain development. "Although it is unwise to overgeneralize on research that is still in development, researchers have found that girls have more neural connections between both sides of their brains and a better developed left brain than boys. It is in the left side of the brain that language activity occurs" (Spence, 2005, p. 11). Michael Gurian (2002) goes into much greater detail in his book *Boys and Girls Learn Differently*, comparing 35 brain regions and chemicals by gender development. Summing up, he states that the brain of a 5-year-old boy looks like that of a 4-year-old girl, while the brain of a 17-year-old boy looks like that of an 11-year-old girl, with the gap persisting until about the age of 30. If schools consider any of this research credible, the need to differentiate instruction *and* continue explicit reading instruction into the high school years should be apparent.

Differentiation would include a careful look at literature selections. Boys tend to prefer adventure, science fiction, war stories, history, and sports (Spence, 2005). Given choices, they often prefer nonfiction, magazines and newspapers, how-to reading, and biographies. Attention to learning styles would reveal that males need the classroom to be far more interactive, with the opportunity to move around the room. They have a more tactile, hands-on learning style and probably will not enjoy verbal discussions of narratives about emotional situations among characters.

In personal conversation, Albert Herscovitch, coordinator of the Rosscarrock Community and Family Support program in Calgary, described his development of a long-term project to build student capacity in resilience.

One component of the project is a course that was initially developed for middle school males who had problems with anger. The material was so applicable to all adolescents that it is now offered as an elective for both genders. However, Herscovitch discovered that the methodology that was successful for males didn't work as well in groups of girls. Boys did the curriculum as a challenge course, through completion of action projects. Girls, on the other hand, said they didn't want action projects, they just wanted to do the course "by gossip." The initial negative reaction of staff was ameliorated when girls clarified, "No, we mean learn by just talking about the stuff . . . not doing those boy projects."

A STUDENT GETS THE LAST WORD

Choices of reading material and variations between projects and discussions may not seem like major adjustments. But RaShawn, a junior in an urban high school, makes the point that when school leaders show students they respect their opinions in the little things, they send a message of confidence and high expectations that pays off in bigger things too. "When they give us more responsibility than they usually would—other people might call it challenging us—they show that they trust us to accomplish it. Giving us more say in our education means they think we're capable. They trust us to make the right decisions about our learning, about our daily experiences at school" (Cushman, 2005, p. 323).

11

April, Year 1

It's a Match!

"All right. Last time we talked about the survey of what kids were thinking about boring classes and good classes and respect and doing our best. Do you still have that chart, Mike?"

"You bet. I left some blank places in it to see what comes up from the studying the teachers are doing. We had an early dismissal last week, and I stayed around to see what they were doing in professional development. Did anybody else stay with their study group?"

"Sure did. And it was fasc-in-ating! It was almost like a generation gap right there in the middle of the staff conference room."

"Tom! That's about as vocal as you've been. What do you mean by 'generation gap'?"

"Well, they started talking about things they've learned about what makes good classes, and they almost got into an argument. The older teachers talked about someone named Madeline Hunter, and some other people said that's just a lesson plan checklist, and the older ones said, no, it was all kinds of elements to think about in learning and motivation. So they started mentioning some things like connecting with prior learning, and the Madeline Hunter people said that's an anticipatory set, and some other teachers said it's making connections between text and self, and some other people said it's setting the objectives. They claimed that Hunter said you should demonstrate and model things and check for understanding and give kids guided practice before they have to be independent. But they started getting all hung up on what the right terms are."

"You're kidding. What did the youngest teachers talk about?"

"Well, they had some books by a guy named Marzano and some other people and they talked about nine essential things to include in teaching. I wrote them down."

"Most of them sound pretty familiar. Too bad they put homework and practice in there. I guess that takes care of my fantasy that some research would say it doesn't do any good. Then maybe we could have talked them out of it."

"Not a snowball's chance. But they did say that there's certain kinds of homework that help you learn—not just memorizing stuff."

"What's this 'nonlinguistic representations' bit?"

"Well, remember when you did the blah-blah-blah because female students wanted more discussions. Well, this is like doing things *without* words. Not just reading page after page but showing it in a diagram or something."

"Hey, didn't we have something from that survey about kids wanting posters and charts to help them keep track of their learning?"

"Yeah, it's there all right. And it also talks about outlines to get organized. I wonder if that's like 'advance organizers.'"

"I think it is. I borrowed the book, and there are different things like models and graphic organizers to help get ideas organized in your mind. And specific questions you can ask yourself before you start studying so there's a place to put the information."

"That would be cool. What's the thing about generating and testing hypotheses? That sounds like science."

"Well, it is sort of like the scientific process. You think about things you already know, or you watch some experiments and predict what you think will happen or why it would be happening. Then you check it out."

"That sounds a lot more interesting than just waiting for the teacher to tell you and write it down. So they got a list of at least nine things, but they didn't agree on what they are? Or was it what to call them?"

"Well, it gets even more interesting than that. The *really* old teachers said that even before Madeline Hunter, there was this guy named Benjamin Bloom, and they wanted everybody to use this 'Bloom's taxonomy.' It's got these levels of thinking that Mr. Spark was explaining about when they changed the Mission Statement. Remember how they had 'analytical' thinking and they changed it? Because analysis is one of the levels. It goes from knowledge, to comprehension, to application, to analysis, to synthesis, to evaluation."

"OK, so like what's the difference between knowledge and comprehension?"

Teri speaks up in her soft voice. "I can tell you that one for sure. Knowledge is just some facts you know—like what Edison invented and what date. But comprehend means understand. Like get the idea behind electricity."

"OK, so comprehend the idea and apply it, I suppose, and analysis—I get that—like we analyzed the data from the student surveys. What about synthesis and evaluation?"

"Synthesis is like taking different ideas or things you learned from different classes and putting them together so they make more sense, or so it's a newer, bigger idea. And evaluation is deciding if something is true or false, or what's the best decision, and so on. The point was that those teachers were saying kids are bored because classes are all on knowledge and comprehension and there's no challenge to use higher-level thinking skills."

"And . . . that's *another* thing that was in the student comments—about needing challenge."

"All right—so there's these 9 things, and these 6 levels, so we've got 15, right?"

"Well, that's not all. Those two brand new teachers—one's in English and one's in social studies—well, they had a couple other books that they said everybody should read. One sounded like I could have written it— something like 'I read it but I don't get it.' And the other one really made the other teachers groan. It was a question like 'Do I really have to teach reading?' and some of them started getting all antsy about what they went to college for and kids should learn to read in elementary school and all that. But there's seven things in there that sound a lot like the other lists. There's predicting, and . . ."

"We get the picture, OK? So who won? How did it turn out?"

"Well, they decided to think about these different lists of things and come up with a few things they would all agree to work on to improve their classes. So that will be coming up. Stay tuned for the next episode of 'Teacher Wars.'"

"Wow. I wish I was in your group. We didn't have that big of an argument in Relationships group, but there *was* some disagreement. They were reading a book about high schools called *Breaking Ranks II,* and it was talking a lot about breaking up a school into smaller schools so people could know each other. So there would be like three to four schools inside our building instead of just one."

"I'll bet that went over like a lead balloon."

"You're right. They said it would be too complicated, and they would have to teach different courses that they don't know very well and a bunch of other reasons. But that's OK. I don't want to be in a divided-up school myself. I think we're doing pretty well as one. What other ideas were in there?"

"Well, they had a bunch of recommendations about that. Like every student having an adult advocate and a personal learning plan. And there were stories about high schools with advisories instead of just homerooms and having mentors for the ninth graders."

"That would make sense. We discovered how many times ninth graders get in trouble because they don't know the ropes and all the different rules of high school."

"Did they have any other ideas that weren't quite so radical as breaking up our school?"

"Yes. One was to have certain adults work with certain kids all the time they're in high school. I got to thinking that it would make more sense for the four counselors to split up the kids and always have the same ones, instead of each counselor having a certain grade and you change counselors every year."

"Hmm. I guess it does make sense. Makes it kinda hard to trick them, though. I mean, if you have the same counselor all the time, you can't say, 'Oh, gee, I didn't know. Mrs. So-and-So never explained it that way.'"

"Well, Mike, it could be that some of your old middle school tricks aren't going to work anymore."

"That's true. We had one of those Marzano books in the Relationships group too, and it talked about teachers having a blend of cooperation with the kids but still being dominantly in charge. That's what I like. Be personal to us, but don't put up with any nonsense."

"That came up in our Responsibility study group as well. You have to give kids some responsibility, but that doesn't mean just laissez-faire. 'If the teacher gets lah-zay, the kids just get lay-zy.' They laughed pretty good at that one."

"Anyway, that book talked about clear learning goals and flexible learning goals and taking a personal interest in students and responding to students positively even if they got the answer wrong. It really reminded me of the kids' stuff from the survey about choices and not being put down."

"There was another book by the same guy that had a chapter about motivation in it. It talked about why people will work on things or give up on things. Some of it was pretty cerebral, but some of it was just common sense. Like giving students feedback and having tasks that are engaging and letting students propose their own projects. That's like how you made a deal with Mr. Adams about crunching the data, Morris. And Gloria's working on her sculpture in all her free time with Mrs. Paulson."

"Okay, did we hear about every group? I see Mike's been writing on his chart. Did you get some stuff for our problems about boring classes and quality work and respect?"

"I sure did. Some of it I wrote down more than once because it seemed to fit. It makes sense to try some things that will help with learning *and* respect and quality work. Now I'm curious about how it compares to what the students said."

"OK. The acid test. Let's go back to the student chart and highlight the ones that seem the same as the teacher chart."

As Mike began to highlight the needs expressed by students that were also mentioned in the study of research and best practices, the students began to smile and then to cheer.

Morris proudly proclaimed, "Ladies and gentlemen, we have a match!" while Teri whispered, "Maybe this is really going to make a difference for kids who have trouble."

Figure 11.1   Teacher Concerns and Findings

TEACHER CONCERNS	STUDY SAYS . . .
Low test scores	Identify similarities and differences Summarizing and note-taking Homework and practice Nonlinguistic representations Generating and testing hypotheses Cues, questions, and advance organizers Demonstration and modeling Checking for understanding
Poor quality work	Reinforcing effort Providing recognition Setting objectives Providing feedback Give engaging tasks and activities Let students design long-term projects
Lack of student motivation	Activating prior knowledge Reinforcing effort Providing recognition Setting objectives Providing feedback Guided practice Cooperative learning Give engaging tasks and activities Let students design long-term projects Higher levels of thinking: application, analysis, synthesis, evaluation
Lack of respect from students	Blending dominance and cooperation Having clear learning goals Having flexible learning goals Taking personal interest in students Being positive and equitable with students Giving dignity to incorrect responses

QUESTIONS FOR REFLECTION

1. Figure 11.1 summarizes what study groups learned about the areas of teacher concern. How is effective teaching defined in your school? What is the range of knowledge bases scattered among the staff? What efforts have been made to develop a common language to describe powerful instruction?

2. Visualize the classrooms in your school. To what degree do you see student work displayed? How prevalent are visual aids that support the learner, such as posters and charts?

3. In the organization of your school, how many opportunities are there for students to know and interact with the same adult over the entire four years?

4. In Figure 11.2, the student survey responses that match teacher findings are italicized. Perhaps you want to tune in to student voice more intentionally but aren't sure where to start. Is there one aspect of your school where you would have "a match" of both students and staff agreeing that improvement is needed?

5. As you answer these questions in your own thinking, what will you do to check the accuracy of your perceptions with students?

Figure 11.2   Student Concerns Matched to Teacher Findings

STUDENT CONCERNS	SURVEY SAYS . . .

Boring classes—
   – too much lecture
   – teacher even acts bored
   – already know all the stuff
   – too hard and there's no help so tune out
	~ *Have a variety of activities*
	 ~ Show enthusiasm about what they teach
	 ~ *Tell us what we'll learn and why it's important*
	 ~ *Get us into discussions and projects*
	 ~ *Let us work in groups sometimes*
	 ~ *Show us examples and demonstrate what they want us to do*
	 ~ *Check if we understand before giving assignment or going on to next thing*
	 ~ *Get us thinking*
	 ~ *Put up charts and give us outline forms and stuff to get organized*
	 ~ Have a way to get help in class and later

Lack of respect from teachers—
   – put you down when you have ideas
   – act like they think you won't get it anyway
	~ *Ask our ideas and input and use them*
	 ~ *Know our names and something about us*
	 ~ Give expectations with reasons, not just threats

Don't do my best because it's not relevant Can't do my best because there's no help when you need it	~ *Do my best when teacher cares about me and shows belief in me* ~ *Teacher gives some options so I feel like it's my best work* ~ There's a good reason I should be able to know or do what they are demanding ~ I can get help when I'm stuck so I can keep going

CONTENT FOR CONSIDERATION

The Classics: Bloom and Hunter

The work of Madeline Hunter still draws interest, as witnessed by the sales of her son's update (Hunter, 2004). I recently asked David Sousa, author of many titles on brain research (1999, 2001, 2002a, 2002b, 2003, 2005, 2006a, 2006b; Sousa, Nielsen, Zionts, Thurlow, & Bender, 2003), whether the new technologies had discovered anything Hunter had overlooked or contradicted anything that she taught. His answer, as I suspected, was that the use of new imaging methods continues to confirm her thoughts about learning. Her insights on motivating students through interest, meaning, novelty, questioning, feeling tone, and the knowledge of results that we now link to formative assessment remain cutting edge. And her guidance about dignifying student errors is totally relevant to today's emphasis on cultural sensitivity and student efficacy.

Benjamin Bloom's taxonomy of educational objectives is also a classic that should be part of every teacher's knowledge base (Bloom, 1956). Challenging students to higher levels of thinking is repeatedly cited as a factor in student motivation and engagement. With the renewed emphasis on relationships and connectedness and core values, it's important to remember that Bloom and Krathwohl's overall work encompassed not only the cognitive domain but also the stages of development in the affective and psychomotor domain (Bloom, Krathwohl, & Masia, 1964).

More recently, Bob Marzano and colleagues have used a meta-analysis approach to synthesize findings from a wide range of research on "what works" in schools (Marzano, 2003), in classroom instruction (Marzano et al., 2001), and in classroom management (Marzano, 2003). Students are motivated when the objectives are clear and attainable, support is available, and students receive specific and timely feedback on which they can act to improve their own progress.

In order for schools to apply these findings in effective ways, teachers must have the opportunity to know their learners. For example, a teacher can't follow Hunter's (2004) advice to connect with their prior knowledge and experience without some diagnosis of their current knowledge and an understanding of their life experiences. The second cornerstone strategy presented in *Breaking Ranks II* (NASSP, 2004) affirms this need: "Connections With Students: Increase the quantity and improve the quality of interactions between students, teachers, and other personnel by reducing the number of students for which any adult or group of adults is responsible" (p. 6).

In the middle school movement, dividing students into "houses" was a way of reducing the number of teachers that were part of each student's day. In the high school reform movement, development of smaller "schools within schools" such as themed academies seeks to accomplish the same end. In settings where leaders cannot create acceptance for these dramatic changes, closer connections must be developed in other ways.

Adult Advocates

Breaking Ranks II (NAASP, 2004) presents some of these possibilities in their recommendations that "[e]very high school student will have a Personal Adult Advocate to help him or her personalize the educational experience" and that "[e]ach student will have a Personal Plan for Progress that will be reviewed often to ensure that the high school takes individual needs into consideration and to allow students, within reasonable parameters, to design their own methods for learning in an effort to meet high standards" (p. 18). Personal advocates may take the form of counselors, administrators, coaches, and teachers who accept that role for a small number of students over the entire four-year span of the student's time in their school. A major purpose of advisory programs is to connect a small group of students with a nurturing adult on an ongoing basis. In these settings, students can develop and track their progress on four-year plans for their learning and add a fifth-year plan to launch themselves toward their postsecondary goals.

Personal Plans for Progress

The Franklin Pierce School District in Washington State created a model called Navigation 101 that is being adopted and adapted throughout the state (Washington OSPI, 2004b). First, school leaders confronted data—about their dropout rate, about the higher levels of skill needed in the job market, and about the gap in their students' achievement and life outcomes based on poverty and race. "These leaders were looking for ways to motivate students to learn as if their lives depended on it—because, of course, they do" (p. 6).

School leaders then identified specific knowledge and skills that every student "needs to master in order to take charge of his or her own education, career, and life" (p. 6). These included how to understand their own abilities and learning styles, how to interpret their assessment results, how to access information about career choices, how the K–20 system works, and even how to fill out big forms such as the forms to apply for financial aid for college. A guidance curriculum was developed, and all teachers at both the middle and high school level were trained to deliver it. Navigation 101 classes meet twice a month, and each high school teacher leads a class of about 20 students. On these days, the schedule is modified as it would be for an assembly. These classes stay together throughout their four-year high school career, and the teacher is the "Personal Adult Advocate" for those students. Students keep portfolios that include their assessment results, logs of career exploration activities, documentation of 30 hours of required community service, student plans for high school and postgraduation life, and their transcripts.

When students realized the course work they would need to meet their goals, they began to sign up for more challenging classes, such as chemistry, physics, and precalculus. The school had to respond to increased enrollment in these classes by changing its approach to scheduling—and finding ways to offer what students were requesting. They also had to find ways to provide tutoring to help students be successful with challenges they had simply avoided before.

Counselors

As the role of teachers has changed to provide "guidance" through their Navigation 101 groups, the role of counselors has changed considerably. They retain responsibility for the mental health and social services functions, but these have become more structured and defined, and they serve more as brokers of services than direct providers. Counselors now are engaged in monitoring system performance, collecting and analyzing data, identifying emerging problems, and facilitating teams to find solutions. This has moved counselors from the typical bystander role to one of active participants and essential resources in the school improvement process.

The critical role of school counselors is also described by Ruth Johnson (2002) in *Using Data to Close the Achievement Gap*. In their roles related to advising and scheduling, they serve as the schools' gatekeepers. Through conscious or subconscious assumptions about who "will be able to handle" particular courses, far-reaching decisions are made that close windows of opportunity for students. Johnson includes helpful examples of ways to gather data and examine the practices of the counseling office at the same time that teachers are analyzing their classroom practices.

A STUDENT GETS THE LAST WORD

> If students knew when they woke up in the morning that they were going to a school where their opinions affected how the school ran, how their teachers acted toward them, and that what they had to say really mattered in what changes were made in the school—they would really come. It wouldn't just be an education that processes them, but one that they could affect and shape to benefit the student body.
>
> —RaShawn (cited in Cushman, 2005, p. 323)

12 May, Year 1

Kick-Off Assembly—All Thumbs Up

"**M**r. Spark, why are you lookin' so bummed? You don't have your usual smile the last couple days. What's eatin' at ya?"

"Oh, Morris, I'm just really disappointed. It's been bothering me ever since we finished the state tests a couple of weeks ago. I was helping the test coordinator get them all boxed up, and we flipped through some of them because the teachers said kids didn't really try to do well. I couldn't believe it. You could tell they just went down the answer sheet making designs with where they put the bubbles. And some students didn't write anything at all in the boxes for constructed responses. A few even wrote nasty comments. I can't believe a student in my school would write 'screw you' on a test booklet."

"Ouch. That's rude. That would make me mad, not just bummed."

Mr. Spark grimaced and rubbed the back of his neck. "OK. I'll be honest. That *was* my first reaction. I was royally ticked off. I thought to myself that I treat you kids pretty well and why would you not even show up on test days or not even try?! It seemed like a real kick in the pants. But my wife, Judy, always says not to take things so personal, so I tried to get past that. I guess I went from mad to sad."

"Well, Mr. Spark, if you don't mind my saying so, when I took the test last year, I didn't know it was so important to you. It's the 'state' test, so it sounds like something from far away that doesn't really affect us and isn't very important. And, well, I hate to be a narc, but the teachers don't really take it seriously either."

"Tell me more, Morris. Don't mention any names of teachers—that's not what this is about. But what made you think the teachers didn't take it seriously?"

"Well, they did say 'Do your best,' but it was sorta like 'Do your best to just get through it' instead of 'Do your very best to show what you know and what a good school we have.' And some of them complained about it being a waste of time when they could be teaching their curriculum. And one even said, 'The state can make us give the test but they can't really do anything to us if we don't pass.' So, wow, I had no idea this was so important to you."

"Well, Morris, it's important to you too. When some of the universities look at your grades, they also look at whether those grades came from a school ranked high in academics or low in academics and so on. They have a formula, and one thing they include now is the state assessments. A good GPA from a school that isn't considered good in academics doesn't have as much value."

"Yikes. That's important. But who knew? Mr. Spark, I think you should bring this up with the Responsibility group. Because it's just plain irresponsible to blow off a test—whether you're going to go to college or not. You should still put out your best quality work on everything. Joe and Mike can talk about it there because Joe's the big university preppie and Mike's aiming for the technical school, so there's two points of view built right in. You could make some plans for next year—to get everybody here and to get them to do their best. But . . . Mr. Spark, you might need to get on the teachers a little bit too."

"Yeah, you're right. You know how I hate being the tough guy, but I'm going to have to deal with it."

"Comes with the territory of principal, huh? Sometimes it has to be 'no more Mr. Nice Guy.'"

"Morris, sometimes you astound me with your insights. I think you'd make a good principal yourself someday."

"Well, the truth is, I've been thinking about maybe being a teacher at least. Looking at some of the stuff the teachers were studying for professional development and the school improvement plan—I think I could do that stuff, and it would be great to help kids get going in life."

The gymnasium is bursting with every student and staff member of Knownwell High School. The stage is set up, the basketball hoops are raised, and the technology is in place to project the proceedings onto the wall so all can see clearly. It's not graduation yet. But it *is* a commencement. It is the formal kickoff of the Knownwell High School Improvement Plan.

On stage are Mr. Spark, Miss Pope, Morris, Joe, and the four counselors. Mr. Spark begins with a review of the activities of the past year and the many ways in which students and staff have worked together to think about making a good school even better. They have wordsmithed a

Mission Statement and discussed its true meaning. They have worked in homerooms to contribute to a set of Collective Commitments. They have participated in data in various ways—making graphs, discussing results, responding to surveys, and analyzing survey responses. They have volunteered to work with teachers in study groups and learn about what the best schools do and decide some things to try in the coming year.

"Today, we are outlining all those steps and the strategies that will be put in place next year. Joe is here as your official leader, president of the Student Council. Thank you for your leadership, Joe." The senior class breaks into a chant of "Joe—Joe—Joe—Joe." Then stops immediately when Mr. Spark raises his hand.

"There are also some *un*official leaders in our school that I want you to meet. Morris is here on the stage, and out there among you are four other individuals I want to thank. Please stand as I call your name."

As Mr. Spark calls their names, Morris steps forward, and Teri, Tom, Gloria, and Mike rise hesitantly to their feet. Mr. Spark continues, "Ladies and gentlemen, these five young people have taught me a lot this year. Their lunch table has been an ad hoc unofficial advisory group for me. I have always tried to make this a student-centered school, but I have never had as many ideas for how to include the voices of students in its leadership as they have suggested this year. Please help me thank them for their leadership."

The silence of surprise at the hitherto unknown students that Mr. Spark identified as leaders is replaced by applause. This time it is underclassmen and underrepresented students who are the loudest.

Mr. Spark continues. "One of our first tasks this year was to think about what our school stands for and what we believe is important to contribute to our world—the world inside our school, and the world outside the school that represents your future. You have seen this Mission Statement before and held discussions about it. Today I want to present this large plaque that will hang in our Commons to keep us constantly reminded of our Mission. Just as in all your sports, when your coaches tell you to keep your eyes on the ball, we must always keep our eyes on these values and goals. I am going to ask the staff to read this statement together."

**The mission of Knownwell High School is
to provide diverse and challenging learning experiences
in a mutually respectful environment
and to assure that all students
master essential skills,
produce high quality work,
and practice critical thinking and responsible citizenship.**

"You also worked as informal groups and then through the formal student governance structure to establish a set of Collective Commitments as a student body. Your promises are as important as ours. This plaque will also be hung in the foyer. Joe, please lead the student body in repeating the three Collective Commitments."

Although some eyes rolled and some shoulders shrugged, students replied in unison:

> **Respect others.**
> **Respect our place.**
> **Respect our chances.**

"Thank you. Through our work this year, we identified three areas in which we want to make changes. They are directly related to our Mission Statement. We have affectionately referred to them as the five R's. Our Mission Statement says 'master essential skills,' so we've called that the three R's for short. Our Mission talks about being mutually respectful, so we've worked on the R of relationships. And our Mission talks about high quality work, critical thinking, and citizenship, all of which comprise responsibility. We are now going to hear from staff and student leaders about changes we will be making to move us forward. Representing the three R's, here is Miss Pope."

"Ladies and gentlemen, I want to begin by apologizing to you and commending you. My apology is for underestimating your knowledge and insights about important aspects of teaching and learning. One of the most significant ah-ha's of my career occurred this year when Mike showed me a chart that illustrated how students' opinions and desires for their classes matched up with what research on learning tells us as professionals. I have saved up money to fly away to conferences when I could have gathered a group of young people around me to learn about improving my teaching. I also want to commend so many of you who added time to your days to meet with us and talk about how we can improve our school. The seeds you planted by your participation in the democracy of our community will grow to make our world a better place.

"My purpose here is to introduce the strategies we will be putting in place to improve learning in our school. As you look at us as a staff, you will notice that we are a range of ages and skin colors and hair colors—some natural and some not so. If you can have purple hair now and then, why can't I have red?"

After the laughter subsided, she continued: "We have gone to different universities and been trained in our specialty content areas more than we were trained in how to design instruction, so we had a lot of different knowledge bases to draw from. I am proud to say that your teachers have been able to agree on five aspects of powerful teaching that we will all be focused on next year:"

Five Elements of Powerful Teaching
- High Expectations
  - clearly stated
  - consistently enforced
- Important Curricular/Content
  - standards-based
  - summarized regularly
- Student-Centered Lessons
  - active participation
  - options available
- Challenging Material
  - high on Bloom's taxonomy
  - supported with help
- Frequent Assessment and Feedback
  - teacher, peer, and self-assessment
  - knowledge of progress

As each item appeared on Miss Pope's PowerPoint slide, student reaction was mixed. "Active participation" with "options available" was approved with applause. "Challenging Material" was met with groans. "Supported with help" was greeted with sighs of relief.

Miss Pope continued: "In terms of providing help, we have begun work on a ninth-grade course that we will call Power Reading, but the schedule for next year is already too tight, and we have a number of things to work out, so that may not happen until the following year. In the meantime, we will make a commitment to provide some practice in every class period and check on who needs help. We are flexing our schedules so that each department will have one teacher who starts early each day for a 'skinny' period before school and one who stays later for a short period after school.

"To help *us* help *you* learn, we will be here the day after you're already out on summer vacation, reviewing these five elements we just showed you and working on how to change some of our lessons and assignments to incorporate higher levels of thinking.

"We also discovered from your comments and looking at our student achievement data that reading informational content—like your textbooks—is different from most reading you have done so far in school. Yes, I know you're thinking, 'like DUH.' We will be having a speaker come in August to help us learn strategies for reading and thinking in all subject areas, so we can build in some of that support right within our classes. Please be patient with us. Back in the days when we went to college, they said, 'Learn to read in Grades 1–3 and after that read to learn,' so we really didn't know about all this. These are the things we will be working on as far as the first three R's. Now we will hear from Joe regarding responsibility."

As Joe steps to the microphone, he turns toward Miss Pope and applauds. "Ladies and gentlemen, we should be proud of our teachers for being willing to set goals in front of all of us and learn new things themselves. A lot of people talk about lifelong learners, and I hope you know that is what we just saw here. Now we have a responsibility to respond to the strategies they are working on. It comes under 'respect our chances.' We have a responsibility to ask when we need help and to take advantage of the before- and afterschool support that teachers are going to provide by flexing their schedules around to be available. We also have some other kinds of responsibility that we will be working on. For example, we are working with Mr. Spark and some teachers to get just one set of classroom rules so ninth graders don't find it so confusing when they start the year. The rules will match up with the Collective Commitments, and we will all have a responsibility to make sure every student understands and follows them. We can't depend on just the teachers to make this a community—we have a responsibility to hold ourselves accountable for our commitments. We seniors will be graduating, and we depend on the rest of you to keep this school a safe and happy place for yourselves and the new freshmen.

"There are two other areas of responsibility that I want to mention. You might not like hearing this one, but it's important and I want the ninth graders to really listen up. And I hope some of you 10th graders will be hanging your heads. Our principal and teachers are worried about what the results of the state test are going to be, because some of you cut school on test days or just fooled around and didn't take the test seriously. Now, whether we think that's how we should be judged or not, people in town here and around the county and the state look at those results and they form opinions about our teachers and about us. Next year, Mr. Spark is going to be talking more to teachers and to students about this. I just want to say that for the next four years while I'm in college, the reputation of this school I went to will affect me, and I want this school to get credit for how good a place it is. So—respect our place by letting people know that we do learn a lot here.

"Now, for the third area of responsibility that we're going to be working on. This is responsible citizenship shown through participating in leadership in our school. We currently have a Student Senate that consists of people elected from each class—freshmen, sophomores, juniors, and seniors. This turns out to be a small group, and through the student involvement that Mr. Spark started this year, we realize that it doesn't represent all student interests in the school. So starting next year, there will also be a Student House of Representatives. Any group that gets the signatures of at least 30 students will be granted a seat in the House of Representatives and can be represented on committees to plan student activities and so forth during the year. When we say respect each other, that means we need to know and hear from each other—every one of us.

"And now, since I'll be graduating and moving on, I want to pass the torch to Morris, who started a lot of this by bugging Mr. Spark all the time. He's going to talk about some things that will be happening in terms of the fifth R—relationships."

Morris steps toward the microphone with a battered file folder in his hand, and the secretary in the front office remembers his shuffling, stammering request for a few file folders some months before. She thinks about the transformation as he begins.

"Ladies and gentlemen, I—uh—have never given a speech before. So if I just sort of read these points, I hope that will be OK. Number 1: We found out that there are a lot of important things that students can talk about, and we learned that students can also help each other with their work and stuff. So—Number 1—we are going to add 10 minutes to every homeroom period and start making it more like an advisory where we talk things over and make plans. This is the first year to do that, so we aren't quite sure how it will work, but we will talk about it after a few months.

"Number 2: We found out that a lot of ninth graders have trouble getting used to this place when they first come here and don't always know the rules or where to go with questions. So—Number 2—we are starting a ninth-grade mentor program. I'm going to be working with Mrs. Halverson on this. She has already talked to the two middle schools that mostly send kids here. We have a list started of juniors who would be mentors next year, and we want more names, so please talk to her. She has the dates of when we will get trained and when we would meet our new ninth graders. Please participate.

"Number 3: We learned from some data that there's a lot of kids who don't feel like they are connected to any particular person in the school. We know that there's a lot of adults who can relate well to kids, and we'll keep working on that next year. But for now, there is one change we are going to make so there's one person that people will know for four whole years. Would the counselors please stand up? OK, please give them a round of thanks for being your counselors this year. Now, Number 3 is that instead of a different counselor every year going up in the grades, the counselors will have alphabetical groups of students. That way, you will have the same counselor all the way to graduation, and other people in your family will have the same counselor and counselors will get to know our parents better too. So get ready to meet your new counselors. If your last name is A–F, please greet your new counselor, Mrs. Halverson."

As each counselor was introduced to the group of students he or she would serve, it was clear that some students were feeling a sense of loss in the change. Mr. Spark returned to the microphone for his concluding comments.

"Some of you are feeling right now what we will all feel at some point in the coming year. Change is hard. But change is also growth and learning, and that's what we are all about. I'm making a deal with you to keep learning everything I can about making this the best school it can be. Give me a big thumbs-up if you accept my offer. Now, Miss Pope talked about the learning and growing the teachers are tackling. Teachers, do you accept the deal? Big thumbs-up. Students, Joe and Mo here have talked about responsibilities to be mentors, to uphold the Collective Commitments, to include more voices in student leadership, and to represent our school well with quality work and best effort. Do you accept your part of the deal? Let's see the big thumbs-up around this great group of young people.

"Thank you. Now go forth—respecting others, respecting this place, and respecting the chances before you."

QUESTIONS FOR REFLECTION

1. High-stakes assessments have proponents and opponents at every level—classroom, school, district, state, and national. Regardless of opinion, they are a reality that we must address in ethical and responsible ways. What is the prevailing position in your school, and in what ways is it directly and indirectly communicated to students? In addition to academic preparation, how is the attitudinal and motivational context for testing created in your school? What roles and messages are played out by principal, staff, parents, and students?

2. The end of the school year created a natural time for Knownwell High School to celebrate the work of students and staff and kick off plans for the future. What is your next window of opportunity to highlight progress and initiate change? Will you be bold or cautious? Who will be your audience? Why?

3. Review your school's goals and improvement plans. Now compare them to the district, school, and individual staff members' professional development plans. Are they closely aligned, loosely related, or a fragmented potpourri? How can you help participants synthesize and apply what they are learning so they can move forward together to implement your plans and improve student performance?

4. As you answer these questions in your own thinking, what will you do to check the accuracy of your perceptions with students?

CONTENT FOR CONSIDERATION

In its assembly to introduce the school improvement plan, Knownwell High School used a collective thumbs-up to affirm support for the changes ahead. One report included in *The Productive High School* (Murphy et al., 2001) described a level of "school membership in which the student and school exchange commitments" (Wehlage, Rutter, Smith, & Lesko, 1989, p. 120). Such commitments are centered on behaviors that show respect, support, and concern for one another. "Belonging and membership are important because they provide opportunities for students to feel special" (Wilson & Corcoran, 1988). When students see principals, teachers, and counselors commit to new learning and changes of practice, they realize that learning is a mutual commitment.

Flexibility and Support for Student Learning

Students realize the depth of that commitment when a school makes changes in its structure and schedule and adds provisions to help struggling learners. *Breaking Ranks II* (NASSP, 2004) emphasizes the importance of such moves in Recommendation 15: "High schools will develop flexible scheduling and student grouping patterns that allow better use of time in order to meet the individual needs of students to ensure academic success" (p. 5). *The Productive High School* (Murphy et al., 2001, p. 172) reports a variety of techniques used to accommodate student needs, including intensive mentoring or tutoring programs that occur during the regular school day or after school. Schools also alter schedules to offer flexible afternoon or evening programs for students who work during the day. Effective high schools find ways to incorporate flexibility into the classroom itself through use of a variety of instructional strategies and through a dedication to patiently explain and re-explain information that students don't grasp readily. Flexibility also occurs when schools open before the regular school day and stay open long after the school day ends so that students have a place to do academic work in a conducive environment or meet in social groups and school-sanctioned club activities.

Concerns about the achievement of low-performing students also prompt close examination of the factors related to achievement gaps (Goodwin, 2000). Based on a series of Diversity Roundtables conducted by Mid-Continent Research for Education and Learning (Goodwin, 2000), six factors were identified from a synthesis of over 300 reports and documents. They include (1) weak or inappropriate curricula, (2) ineffective instruction, (3) disengaging classroom discourse, (4) poor student self-concept, (5) unsuccessful adjustment to school culture, and (6) prejudice. Guidance for policymakers intent on closing achievement gaps included

- Providing all students with rigorous curricula. At the secondary level, minority and immigrant students are too often relegated to

non-college-bound tracks. And in those classes, there are few cultur-
ally relevant topics and examples to inspire and engage them.

- Helping teachers improve instruction. Teachers need to use a variety
  of approaches and learn about students' cultures so that they can
  use examples, vignettes, scenarios, and aphorisms familiar to their
  students.
- Providing support to students. High-poverty, high-performing
  schools regularly assess students, identify those who need help, and
  provide afterschool and summer school sessions to increase instructional time. Newcomer centers for immigrant students offer intensive instruction in English and orientation to American culture and
  schooling as a transition to regular classroom settings.
- Creating smaller classes and school units. The change to "house"
  identification in middle schools is provided as a useful model.
- Increasing parent involvement. Bringing health care, counseling, and
  other social service representatives to the campus is offered as one
  way to attract hesitant parents.
- Identifying and fixing ways low performance is manufactured. The
  rate of teacher turnover in low-performing schools results in an
  overrepresentation of inexperienced teachers, less skilled in pedagogy
  and ill prepared for the cultural differences they encounter. District
  support through coaching by master teachers and additional time
  for planning and collaboration are essential.
- Establishing strong, yet fair, accountability. Although standard
  methods of reporting high-stakes assessment results are unavoidable,
  it is imperative that districts also measure students' growth from their
  starting point and judge schools by the value they add to student
  achievement.

Ninth-Grade Transition Programs

Concerns about adjustment to school culture relate directly to the
achievement of students from diverse backgrounds but also affect all
students making the passage from elementary, middle, or junior high settings into the high school environment. Transitions are always hard, but
few are as difficult in the life of teenagers as that of starting at a new high
school. Responses reported in *The Productive High School* (Murphy et al.,
2001) include orientation programs for freshmen and other new students.
These new students may be paired with peer helpers or buddies, provided
extra time with counselors, hosted on school tours, invited to parent
orientation nights, and interviewed about interests in school activities.
Peer mentoring, peer mediation, and peer tutoring have all been linked
with enhanced academic performance (p. 164). One specific program, the
Learning Resource Lab, is described as a combination of study hall, homeroom, and advisory group (p. 167). Provisions include adult tutoring, a

conflict resolution workshop, an introduction to the library media center, a learning styles inventory, free reading every day, study skills and note-taking workshops, and an introduction to clubs and organizations. After three years of implementation, the school has documented that freshmen have fewer failing grades, fewer discipline referrals, fewer suspensions, fewer absences, and a more positive attitude toward school.

At City College High School in Baltimore, Maryland, the Summer Bridge program is designed to familiarize incoming students with the school routine, orient them to the layout of the building, and clarify expectations and the approach teachers use in the classroom (NASSP, 2004, p. 134). In addition, bonds are formed through Outward Bound-style team-building activities, including a field day and picnic. Counselors and administrators teach sessions during the summer program so that incoming students have met them under less formal conditions than the usual school year. Counselors meet with students about tentative schedules, which are sent home to parents for confirmation. From this initial schedule, personal plans for progress are begun by each student.

At Maine East outside Chicago (Lampert, 2005), the needs of freshmen became apparent when leaders checked their data and discovered that a sizable number of first-year students were unable to successfully adjust and pass their classes. In response, a freshman advisory program was developed in which sophomore, junior, and senior student mentors provide academic and social guidance to younger students. A curriculum was developed, and mentors deliver it in weekly sessions under the supervision of adult staff. Prospective mentors are selected on the basis of their people skills and are trained through direct instruction and role playing. Activities focus on attachment, achievement, and awareness (of mental health issues and healthy life decisions). Reported results include a decrease in first semester failure rate from 37 percent in 2002–2003 to 23 percent in 2004–2005. Changes have also occurred in attitudes of both staff and incoming students. Some staff initially denigrated the idea that so much time and attention should be focused on this group of students. And the program's first participants were highly resistant to having their academic progress monitored and to participating in advisory activities. Students now report that the program is helpful for their first year of high school and "also helps us with all the stresses of everyday life" (Lampert, 2005, p. 62) and that they like being able to do their homework in a relaxed place where they can get help.

A STUDENT GETS THE LAST WORD

Although the teenage façade may seem to belie the point, high school students want to learn, and being able to get help with learning is a factor in whether and how hard they will try.

She is so patient. Last semester I was having real difficulty in under-standing. . . . She sat with me three days after school. I kept saying it was impossible, but she stuck with me, and finally I got it. She was as happy as I was! (Platt, Tripp, Ogden, & Fraser, 2000, p. 194)

September, Year 2

Fresh Start, Staff Retreat

"Hey, Mr. Spark. How are things going? All ready for the first day of school?"

"Well, Morris, we're almost all set for Tuesday after this holiday weekend. I'm trying to decide whether to start with an assembly for everybody or just for the new ninth graders."

"What if you did an assembly with the ninth graders and us mentors? We've had a couple of activities with them, and they've seen you, but you haven't really talked to them in person. And it would make us all, like, partners in starting the school year."

"I like that idea, Morris. But what about the sophomores and juniors? Do you think they'll remember everything we went over at the end of last year?"

"True, a good review never hurts. Plus there might be some new kids that moved in over the summer. What if you talk over the intercom and give a short version and then have the teachers have a little discussion in the advisories? That would start out using the advisories for real topics. Besides, you'd have a pretty hard time topping that assembly we had last May. It would be sort of anticlimactic."

"I like that idea, Morris. I'll get it together. Now what about the Table Ten group? Are you going to be having lunch together this year?"

"Well, it's going to be harder now that we're seniors. Our schedules are a little different, and Mike might be busy with House of Representatives, and Gloria is working on more pieces of sculpture. Mrs. Paulson said she's actually good enough to have a show at a gallery downtown. And I'll be working with Mrs. Halverson on the mentoring program. But I worked all summer to get a laptop, and we're going to chat on the Internet and then set up some times to get together when there's important stuff to talk about."

"It sure didn't take Mike long to get 30 signatures for Skateboarders' Club. It made him the first new member of student government here. We're headed in the right direction getting more student voices into the mix."

"Right. Now, uh, I'm wondering about a couple more things if you have time."

"Sure, Morris. What's on your mind?"

"Well, you were real bummed out last spring about how the state test scores would come out because kids didn't really try, so I was wondering if you got the results yet."

"Yes, Morris, I've had a look at the preliminary reports. They're about the same as last year, so thank goodness we didn't go down. But I sure think we could do better. I think we have the best school in the county, but I'd like to be able to prove it."

"So, did you tell the teachers that? Is it true that you kinda got on them a bit."

"Why, Morris, what are you referring to? Who have you been talking to?"

"Mr. Spark, you know you can't keep secrets. It's public information that you had a staff retreat. It's not like anybody has been talking a lot, but I get a few little comments from Mrs. Halverson, and Tom hears a few little comments from the football coaches talking during practice, and Teri is already working on her learning plan with Mrs. Donnelly, and we—uh—put some pieces together. You did tell them that they should be more positive about the test, didn't you?"

"Well, I pointed out that we need to model the same responsibility we talk to students about. And I said that we have a great atmosphere for people getting along, but now we need to add some stronger academic expectations as well."

"Right—and that's all, huh? As usual, you're being humble. So I'll tell you what we think happened that we put together from the various things we heard. You gave the teachers a big pep talk, and they all stood in a circle and said they were going for it. Isn't that true?"

"Well, Morris, that just might be. You'd have to ask them if you wanted to be sure. The point is—we'll see if there are any changes in classrooms this year. Then we'll know whether anything significant happened or not."

"OK. But let me just say—if you *did* sort of lay it out for the teachers, and *if* you did say they should model what they want from us, then we say thank you. Because it means you really expect everybody to do their part."

"I do mean that, Morris, and that means me as well. I'll need to show I'm trying something different too."

"Hey, Morris, how was the first day of school for you?"

"It was awesome, sir. When you went over the Mission Statement and the Collective Commitments with the ninth graders, they were just sitting on the edge of their seats. And when you gave the common rules for classes, they were so relieved. Then when you had us turn to each other so mentors and mentees could talk about things, they took out their schedule and wanted to know about specific teachers and who's really a stickler and how to figure out what they want. Then later they were in their advisories, and each teacher went over the same rules as you did. I think they're a lot more confident than they were the first time we got together."

"And how were your own classes, Morris? As a senior, it's important you have a good year."

"Mr. Spark, I have to believe what I heard about you and the staff retreat. Because I tell you, the first day was never like this before. Since the rules are consistent and got taken care of in advisories, each one of my teachers went right to the course syllabus. They talked about state standards and what colleges will be expecting and told us which ones their class would help us with. And they went through the textbook—like showing us which chapters match the weeks of the syllabus. My social studies teacher even divided us up, and each little group looked at a different chapter and then we went back to our first groups and talked about how our chapters were set up. So now we know how the book is organized, and when we have to read a chapter, we'll look through the whole thing first and then check the headings and do some other stuff to get us ready. I never really had trouble with my textbooks, but I'll get a lot more out of it now. And for somebody who has trouble reading or dreads getting started, this will really help them."

"You made my day, Morris! That's called 'using text forms and features to access text,' if you want the teacher-talk for it. It's one of the things we learned in our August inservice. I am so glad to hear it's being applied."

"Well, you know, Mr. Spark, application *is* one of the higher thinking skills, and I think you *did* tell teachers to model for us."

"How did you remember the levels of thinking skills, Morris?"

"Oh, you should know—I didn't really remember them. But I'll be able to soon, because you know very well they're posted in every room. And those five elements of powerful teaching are in every room also. You gave out those posters, didn't you?"

"Well, whatever . . . I'm just glad to get an answer to the question I had—whether kids would see any difference in classes this year."

"Yeah, you got your answer all right, and you're getting the student voice. But you might have to start watching yourself—*whatever* is one of *our* words."

QUESTIONS FOR REFLECTION

1. What provisions are made in your school for ninth graders and new sophomores, juniors, and seniors?

2. What happens in classes on the first day of school? Is it all about rules or about being successful learners?

3. Students put together bits and pieces and create "stories" about what goes on among staff and in their school. (Adults do it too.) What's going on in your school that might be the stuff of stories? What are they? Is clarification or correction needed?

4. Mr. Spark waited through a year of school improvement planning and increased student involvement before directly challenging his staff with high expectations for their performance. Was this good pacing, or should he have made more overt moves sooner? Why? Why not?

5. As you answer these questions in your own mind, what will you do to check the accuracy of your perceptions with students?

CONTENT FOR CONSIDERATION

Essential Learnings

Cornerstone Strategy #1 of the popular *Breaking Ranks II* (NASSP, 2004) expresses a need to "[e]stablish the essential learnings a student is required to learn in order to graduate, and adjust the curriculum and teaching strategies to reach that goal" (p. 6), and the report further states that "[e]ach high school will identify a set of essential learnings—in literature and language, writing, mathematics, social studies, science, and the arts—in which students must demonstrate achievement in order to graduate" (p. 18). Clarity about a core set of concepts and skills that students need is essential, and the level of teacher commitment to align curriculum, instructional resources, and assessment is a distinguishing characteristic of teachers with a major impact on student achievement. Unfortunately, the implication that each individual school makes these decisions in isolation can lead to unintended negative consequences for students. As long as the No Child Left Behind Act requires state standards and tightly aligned state assessments—which in some states are also a graduation exam—high schools must carefully study those academic standards and assessment specifications as they develop course offerings and the attendant curriculum. A high school, a subject area department, or an individual teacher who designs essential learnings in isolation from state standards— and from other high schools in the same district—is putting students, especially mobile students, at risk and is exacerbating one of the factors that contributes to achievement gaps among subgroups of students.

Advisory Programs

A series of questions about how well your school serves each student raises the query, "Are the aspirations, strengths, and weaknesses of each student known by at least one faculty member or other member of your staff? How do you ensure the staff member uses that information appropriately to help the student become successful in all classes and activities?" (NASSP, 2004, p. 2). In response, schools are urged to "[i]mplement a comprehensive advisory program that ensures each student has frequent and meaningful opportunities to plan and assess his or her academic and social progress with a faculty member" (p. 6).

A comprehensive advisory program would actually begin through (a) articulation with middle schools or junior highs that send students to the high school and (b) the development of transition plans for incoming ninth graders. Successful advisory programs involve development of guidelines and expectations for staff who will be the advisers, including topics that should be discussed in the small group setting. Advisory time should include opportunities for students to lead discussions about their progress and accomplishments. The advisory period is the venue for development of personal learning plans, which capture students' reflections on aspirations, learning styles, areas for strength and improvement, courses to be taken, and a collection of significant artifacts from academic, service, and extracurricular endeavors.

At Poland Regional High School in Poland, Maine (Allen, 2005), groups of students are assigned to an adviser in "roundtables" that meet for 30 minutes every day. In this model, students meet with the same adviser and classmates through all four years of high school. The advisory is figured into a teacher's assignment as a "fifth class" that requires preparation of activities that help students focus on guiding questions such as "Who am I? Where am I going? How am I doing?" In their advisory, students take career interest inventories and make arrangements for job shadowing as well as celebrating their accomplishments as they move toward graduation.

Advisory programs that are well planned and carefully implemented have had documented benefits (Osofsky et al., 2003), which include increases in test scores, decreases in failing grades, more students taking college entrance exams, improvement in student-teacher relations, and a decline in dropouts.

A STUDENT GETS THE LAST WORD

In history the first day my teacher passed out a paper with a couple of questions about how you learn—like: what type of issues do you have with history, do you like it? That was the first time a teacher seemed to actually care about how a student learns, so she could meet their needs. It made me think about how I learn—I never thought about it before, because I'd never been asked.

—Tiffany (cited in Cushman, 2005, p. 5)

14

October, Year 2

Football Faux Pas, and Just Walking Through

Three young men sit in chairs in the short hallway outside the principal's office, waiting to talk with Mr. Spark. He finishes his telephone call and sighs in disappointment over the situation his colleague in a neighboring high school has just described. "Who could have pulled such a stunt—and why would they let us down like that?" he wonders. He makes a notation to follow up on the report and opens his door to see who is waiting.

"Gentlemen, what can I do for you today?" He realizes that these must all be ninth graders, since he has mastered the names of two but not all three. "Did someone send you to the office?"

"Well, no, sir. Er, not exactly, that is."

"You were sort-of-but-not-exactly sent to the office. Is that what you're saying? Maybe you should start at the beginning."

"Well, we were talking with some of our friends and a couple of the mentors, and we just asked them sort of a 'what if'—like what should somebody do if they knew somebody had done something wrong and then felt bad about it. And they started in about those Collective Commitments, and when you hurt someone, you hurt the whole school. And if somebody does something wrong, they should go to whoever was hurt by it and admit it and figure out a way to make it right if they can."

"That seems like good advice. Was there a specific 'something wrong' that somebody might know about that you were referring to?"

"Yes, sir—and that's why we're here. We figure we hurt you the most and so we have to tell you. We were fooling around at the football game, kinda hanging out after the teams went to the locker room and people were packing up. And the other school, they just sort of left those padded coach chairs sitting out there, and we thought it would be a pretty good souvenir of beating them finally—and—we grabbed a couple and put them in the back of my dad's pickup and took them home."

"You took some property from the other school home with you? And now you don't feel so good about it. What made you change your thinking?"

"Well, at first we thought those Collective Commitments were kind of corny at the start of school. But now we know people here are really serious about them. And if we have promises to respect others and respect our place here, then we should respect other people and *their* place and their stuff. At first, we were thinking it was just a prank on the other coaches, but then we realized that they would probably be talking all over their school, and that would give a bad impression of our school, and it would really hurt you with all you try to do to make this a good school. So we wanted to tell you, and we are going to be taking the chairs back after school."

"You must know that I'm very disappointed that this even happened. As a matter of fact, I did just get off the phone with my buddy who was wondering if I knew anything about some missing chairs. I apologized and told him I'd look into it. That felt pretty bad. On the other hand, I'm very proud of you for learning what Knownwell High School is all about and coming forward. It does show we're making progress in that 'responsibility R' that we talk about. Unfortunately, it's not quite as simple as coming forward and returning the chairs. This amounts to theft, and I don't have any choice under school board policy except to suspend you."

"Yes, sir, we know that. We told our parents this morning that they'd be getting a telephone call from you. But we already feel a whole lot better. And we had one other idea we wanted to ask you about."

"Go ahead. What's on your minds?"

"Well, we were thinking that we should probably do more than just take the chairs back. That's just sort of undoing the wrong thing we did, like canceling a minus up to a zero. We wanted to add something positive so when they talk about Knownwell, they have something else to say."

"What did you have in mind?"

"In social studies, Mr. Soderberg talks about service a lot, and we thought maybe we could volunteer to do some service for their school. Like there's a big event up there on Saturday, and it seemed like maybe we could help out some way."

"Gentlemen, I think that's an excellent idea. I'll go do the paperwork for your suspension, and you can use my phone to call and arrange to return the chairs and talk over the service idea."

"OK. Here are the forms for your parents about your suspension. This is the easiest disciplinary process I've ever had. I didn't even have to track down your parents, because they've all called in and said they know you'll be headed back home. How did your phone call work out?"

"Well, sir, the principal said we should bring the chairs up on Saturday morning. They're going to be having a choir clinic, and they need every chair they can get their hands on for the various groups—and, uh—I mean, I know there's nothing funny about this, sir, but . . . our service is going to be setting up chairs in the morning and taking them back down at the end. I guess what goes around comes around, doesn't it?"

Mr. Spark barely manages to hide a grin as he distributes a suspension letter and a handshake to each young man. "Thank you for coming forward. And don't forget—now I know you real well and I'll be watching you."

"Not a problem. You do your job, but you'll never have to do it with us again. We know what this place stands for now. It's one thing for the teachers to say it. But when our classmates get all over us, well, we won't mess up again."

As Mr. Spark returns to his daily routine and proceeds into the Commons to look, listen, and learn, he realizes that he's just had evidence of one R and wonders about the three R's of learning and how things are going in the relationships arena. For the third time that week, he notices that a ninth grader named Aaron is circling in his peripheral vision. "Is he trying to approach me?" Mr. Spark wonders. He changes direction and accidentally-on-purpose nearly bumps into Aaron.

"Oh, sorry. It's Aaron, isn't it? How are things going here for you?"

"Uh, OK. I—uh—I was—uh—just trying to find something to do until class. I don't eat much and I . . . oh, never mind."

Aaron begins to walk away but Mr. Spark pursues. "Aaron, is there something that you would *like* to do until class? Perhaps there's something that's interesting to you and we could talk about it."

Aaron's face lights up. "Well, I was kind of wondering if there's some place I could maybe play chess. It's something I like to do, but I don't know if anybody else does, or what."

"You know, Aaron, I do have an idea, and maybe I can put something together."

"Well, I think I should do something about it myself if you would just give me an idea where to start."

"Excellent, Aaron. It sounds like all you need is a connection. So here's a hint for you. Mr. Ralston in the media center was a real hotshot chess player back when he was in college."

"Really? . . . It's hard to imagine what teachers used to be like when they were young. I'm going to talk to him."

Three weeks later, Mr. Spark finds a note on his desk from Mr. O'Brien. It's just an update that the House of Representatives is increasing in size. Three more groups have brought the required petition and signatures to have a representative in student government. Mr. Spark smiles when he sees that the most recent addition is the Chess Champs, represented by no other than the skittish Aaron.

Progress on two R's heard from so far, and Mr. Spark begins to think about the Three R's learning focus. A few students have shared examples of different class activities with him. Like Mr. Hofstad showing a bit of *Apollo 13* in his science class to introduce the topic of energy conservation—shutting down systems to save electrical power. But Mr. Spark is also thinking about his statement to Morris that he would need to show he was trying something different also.

Staff meeting is almost over, and Mr. Spark makes his move. "I appreciate the commitment you've made to implement powerful teaching strategies this year and incorporate more of the higher-level thinking activities into your classes. Students have commented on the posters in your rooms, so they are noticing. I want to be sure I notice your efforts as well, so I've worked with the assistant principals and some department heads on our goals for visibility in classrooms. We want our goals to be aligned with the school mission and goals also, so we're going to aim for brief informal visits to 10 classrooms a day, three days a week. And we're just going to take note of the five elements of powerful teaching that we identified together. We'll just use this simple note-taking form and report back to you on the frequency of these strategies we observe. We know we might not be there at the right time to see everything you're doing, but we'll have some rough idea of which are going well and which may be most challenging. Any questions?"

"We always want you in our classrooms. But students might be distracted."

"I think they'll get used to it. Just nod at us and keep right on with your lesson."

"You said it wouldn't be evaluative, but you have a column for the room numbers there. So it seems like you'll be keeping track."

"Well, our intent was to make sure that the three of us don't end up making multiple stops in some rooms and completely missing some others. But I'm willing to talk about it if it's a concern."

"Mr. Spark, we think it's good that you're sharing the focus. I think we should give you a chance and see what comes of it."

"Thanks—anyone else? Well, then, the three of us will give it a try and let you know what does come of it after a month or so."

QUESTIONS FOR REFLECTION

1. The incident regarding theft of a football chair is real, and the students did actually come forward to confess and seek a way to make restitution above and beyond returning the chairs. (I do not know what the exact service was, so I enjoyed the irony of setting up chairs.) Do you believe that a school culture can be strong enough to prompt such action on the part of students? If so, how? If not, why not?

2. Student involvement at Knownwell High School led to increased representation in student government and a wider range of clubs and activities. What percentage of students at your school participate in at least one activity? What are the reasons other students don't?

3. Figure 14.1 shows the chart Mr. Spark and others used on informal walk throughs. Teachers had mixed reactions to the idea of administrators increasing their informal classroom visits and aligning them with the elements of effective teaching. What do you think was behind their questions? How would (or does) this look in your school?

4. As you answer these questions in your own thinking, what will you do to check the accuracy of your perceptions with students?

CONTENT FOR CONSIDERATION

Restorative Justice

Approaches to schoolwide discipline run the gamut from strictly enforced zero-tolerance policies to problem-solving models like peace-making circles, circles of courage, and restorative justice. Although veteran staff in particular may find these measures "soft" and too "touchy-feely," participants often report that face-to-face accountability and restoring what has been damaged, harmed, or hurt is actually far more difficult than just serving out a quota of detentions. Communities are based on social

Figure 14.1   Five Elements of Powerful Teaching

Date of walk-throughs: _____

Room No.	High Expectations —clearly stated, consistently enforced	Important Content— references to standards, summarized	Student Centered— active participation, options	Challenging Material— high Bloom's, help available	Frequent Assessment —feedback from self, peers, teacher; progress noted

relationships, and we want high schools to feel like and function like communities, so it makes sense to consider restorative measures that provide a social process for making things right in ways that strengthen the community rather than ostracizing members. Sarah Studer (2001), a senior at Boulder High School, wrote about her training and experience in restorative justice, which was first implemented as a re-entry exercise for students returning from suspension. She reported that since the program was begun, many suspensions have been avoided, and almost all contracts have been completed. A team of student facilitators work with small groups that usually include three students and an administrator. Conferences are held after school on Mondays. Studer notes that three days off for breaking a rule doesn't always teach offenders how their actions affected others.

It is interesting to note that none of the 31 recommendations in *Breaking Ranks II* (NASSP, 2004) speaks directly to discipline practices as one of the factors associated with a personalized school environment. Perhaps the closest connection is implied in Recommendation 17: "The high school community, which cannot be values-neutral, will advocate and model a set of core values essential in a democratic and civil society" (p. 18).

Walk-Throughs

Accountability is a reality that also affects the adult community in the school. The term *walk-through* has many definitions in various contexts. At Knownwell High School, it is an approach to informal classroom visitation that occurs as an ongoing part of the administrators' instructional supervision. "Principals who do short walk-throughs several times a week often are the most effective principals in a school district. They can help teachers share methods that support student motivation and learning, and they contribute to a school's focus on a direction and vision of success" (Easton, 2004).

As described in *The Learning Principal* (Roy, 2006), walk-throughs consist of a team of observers dispatched to various classrooms where they spend about 10 minutes looking for very specific kinds of evidence. Observers then gather to assemble their information and share what they have learned with the teachers whose rooms have been observed. Whether there are multiple observers participating on a single day or a few observers gathering information on multiple occasions, walk-throughs create a schoolwide picture made up of many small snapshots. They provide an opportunity to

- Reinforce attention on an instructional and learning focus in the school's improvement plan
- Gather data about instructional practice and student learning to supplement other data about school and student performance

- Stimulate collegial conversation about teaching and learning through asking questions about what evidence is and isn't observed
- Learn from other participants through observations, questions, experiences, and perspectives
- Deepen understandings and improve practices through continuous feedback (p. 4)

Additional information on walk-throughs is available in *Powerful Designs for Professional Learning* (Easton, 2004), published by the National Staff Development Council (NSDC), and by visiting *From the Toolbox* in the members-only area of the NSDC Web site, www.nsdc.org. *The Three-Minute Classroom Walk-Through* (Downey, Steffy, English, Fraser, & Poston, 2004) may also prove helpful.

A STUDENT GETS THE LAST WORD

Our school says it cares about all of its students, but then it sends out detention slips without ever talking to a student to see what's going on. They don't take the time to even talk to you. Sure, the school is big, but there are many small ways it could show respect for students. Talking to a kid before sending them to detention for the fifth time is one. (What Kids Can Do, n.d.)

November, Year 2

Plans and Portfolios

Morris meets Mr. Spark in the Commons during arrival time in the morning. He carries the morning newspaper. "Mr. Spark, it says here that now the state wants everybody to have a four-year learning plan and keep a portfolio until they're seniors. I don't think that applies to us seniors now, does it?"

"No, Morris. That's going to be a requirement of the students who are only in eighth grade now, so there's time to implement it."

"Well, I was thinking that it might actually be a good idea to start with the freshmen we have right now, even if it's not a law yet, because I'm mentoring two ninth graders, and they really don't have an idea of how important some things are and that they need to get serious already. The counselors are working on more ways to have relationships and all that, but I think the Responsibility group should take a look at this idea and get it going sooner. It shouldn't be just the counselors keeping track of what you need—it should be us students, and parents too, if we're lucky enough to have them involved."

"Morris, I like your thoughts. Maybe we've waited too long, just starting to talk graduation requirements with the juniors. We did that because everybody took mostly the same things as freshmen and sophomores."

"Well, that 10th-grade test is pretty important, and you said we would need to get better on that—so we should start laying it out with the freshmen right away. And make sure they know what courses they need to take seriously to be ready for it."

"You're exactly right. I was going to get a committee together to start thinking about that for next year, but I think I'll move sooner on it. Thanks for the suggestion."

"Well, if you don't mind my saying so, why do you have to get a committee together? We already have people left from the study groups on responsibility from last year—let's tap into that. You said we would still meet several times this year to keep track of how things are progressing."

"Absolutely right. Mr. O'Brien and Mr. Soderberg were working with that group, and Mike, but Joe has graduated. Ah—I get the point, Morris. You're saying it's time to get some ninth graders into that group to help shape this new requirement. Sometimes it takes me a while, but I'm catching on. I'll start talking it up. Any particular reason you got so interested in this, Morris?"

"Yes, sir, one really big reason. My brother, Norris, is in eighth grade right now. I want you to get this set up right before he comes here. I know they're going to change some boundaries for school attendance, but my mom already has the papers to fill out so he can go here because he's my sibling."

"I can see he's lucky to have you for an older brother, Morris. Just as we are lucky to have you as a student leader."

The Choir Room is full as usual when the entire faculty has its monthly meeting. There are only two items written on the chalkboard:

1. Five Elements of Powerful Teaching

2. Four-Year Plans and Portfolios

"Looks like a real short agenda. Maybe we'll get out of here early."

Mrs. Halverson chides her colleague. "Don't count on it. We have some digging to do on that second topic. But at least we have time to get right to the important stuff."

"Yeah. I have to admit that I sorta miss the old faculty meetings when we could just sit and go over announcements. I didn't use my e-mail much then. Now I know I have to open my e-mail every single day or I won't know what's going on."

"I'm sure interested in finding out whether that walk-through chart really got used and how people will react. Oh, time to start."

"Good afternoon, ladies and gentlemen. Thank you for being here promptly. I know the announcements have been getting out there on your e-mail. If you have any questions, we'll come back to them at the end of the meeting. As you can see, we have just two main topics today. The first will only take a few moments. I appreciate the attitude you showed last month when I introduced the idea of having a focus for informal visits to your classrooms when we drop in briefly, and I promised to bring you some results and check with you as to how it's going from your perspective. During the past month, we weren't able to fulfill our goal of 10 classrooms each on three days each week. You're well aware of all the unexpected things that came up. If we'd met our goal, it would have been a total of 360 walk-through visits. You're right. That's a lot. Three of us times three days times 10 each day times four weeks. That's 360—kinda like getting a full 360-degree look at what's going on. We did manage 240 this month, and here are the results. For example, we saw 158 examples we could identify as clear expectations, so that was observable in 66 percent of our 240 walk-through stops."

Five Elements of Powerful Teaching

Date of walk-throughs: October

No. Visits	High Expectations— clearly stated, consistently enforced	Important Content— references to standards, summarized	Student Centered— active participation, options	Challenging Material— high Bloom's, help available	Frequent Assessment— feedback from self, peers, teacher; progress noted
240	158 66%	120 50%	96 40%	72 30%	48 20%

"We know there's much more happening than we can see in these brief drop-ins. So we make note of it and count it even if we just hear a comment about it or see something in the room connected to it. Like if the objective is written on the board or if students can tell us specifically what they're learning that day, we know it's going on even if we weren't there when you started the lesson. The main purpose for this is to commend you. Even if these numbers don't really capture it, we can tell you that we're seeing a lot more student engagement in classes this fall. And more clarity about what you're teaching and why. Do you have any comments?"

After a short silence, one staff member makes an observation. "I think the ones with lower percentages so far are harder to do. Like you only saw frequent assessment in 20 percent of the walk-through visits. In college, I was taught a lot about how to teach but not much about stuff like formative assessment. Maybe we need to have some professional development on that."

"Good point. Let's give it another month or so, and you talk about this data in your study groups and let me know what you're thinking. We'll take it from there. Keep up the good effort in these five areas."

"Our second topic is Four-Year Plans and Portfolios. As you know, the state has made this a new requirement, starting with the students who are now in eighth grade. I've had some student input that I think really merits our discussion. The suggestion is to get started this year, with these ninth graders as a pilot, so we can give them a heads-up about their next four years. It seems to fit very well with the 'responsibility' aspect of our school improvement plan. There have been many discussions in this room about students taking their high school experience seriously, and I believe we have a good venue here to work with them so they have a clear map through the next four years."

"Are you suggesting they have to make a career choice when they're only ninth graders?"

"No, not at all. But I think they do need to be exposed to the general range of choices after graduation—four-year college, two-year program, military, employment, and so on. And they need to realize which doors they are keeping open or closed by their choices of courses and the amount of effort they put forth."

"In that case, good idea. And I think our parent organization has something similar in mind. They're putting together some booklets or something about maps through high school based on destination. Maybe we could plug them in with this."

"Any objections from anyone? If we're going to introduce it to our freshmen, I'll want to move as soon as possible. There's already a Responsibility group that I've talked with, and they're ready to dive in. My thought is, let's take a new requirement from the state and turn it into lemonade by making it fit our timing and our goals and Mission."

The silent chorus of nods—and absence of objections—gives Mr. Spark all he needs to proceed.

This time it's the auditorium that's full as the ninth graders assemble to hear about something new.

"What's this about a Four-Year Plan? Mine is just to get through it and get on with my life!"

"Doofus. Did it ever occur to you that for four years this *is* our life? You act like it's a sentence you have to serve or something. Why don't you give it a chance? You might be able to make something of it."

Mr. Spark introduces the topic and the first student speaker, who shows a graph of lifetime earnings based on amount of education.

The two in the back row exchange words again. "See, doofus, if you blow this off, you're going to be driving a junker when I get my Mercedes."

A second student presents a list of the kinds of information that are kept on each student—attendance, behavior, grades, participation in activities—and points out that these are factors taken into consideration by employers and admissions offices. "So they are important for your enjoyment of school now, and also for your future. We believe that students should know and also keep track of such important information, so we're now giving you a portfolio and a CD that's already formatted with templates for your own monitoring of some of this information."

After portfolios are passed down the rows, the third student speaker reviews graduation requirements, going over the hard-copy handout in their folders and reminding them that the CD includes a template for keeping track of their fulfillment of these requirements.

Then comes Morris. "There's a fourth aspect of being responsible for your learning that occurs here in school but has long-range impact for you and is significant for our whole school. That is the state test that you will be taking next year in 10th grade. That might seem a long way off, but I can tell you that it's a test you can pass if you get serious in your core classes now and take advantage of the help classes that are going on before and after school. Here's a graph that shows the last few years of our overall scores compared to the county and the state. You'll notice that we're a little ahead of the state every year and pretty much around the average for the county. Last year was pretty embarrassing, because some students didn't take this seriously. We know we're better than the state—think about some of the cities that are in this state and you know we should be ahead of them. And I think we're more than just "average" even in our own county. So I'm challenging the 10th graders to make this line go up, and I'm daring you to do even better because you've had more advance warning. By now you've learned that at Knownwell High School, we have three commitments—c'mon, say them—respect others, respect this place, respect our chances. Show respect for yourself, for our school, and for your future by taking this seriously."

Mr. Spark returns to the microphone and asks, "How many of you have sisters or brothers in seventh or eighth grade right now? Good. You're wondering why I ask that question. Well, I'm admitting to you that we haven't tried this before here, and we'll probably have some glitches in the process as we move forward. So if you get frustrated, please think about those younger brothers and sisters and how much better it will be for them if you help us get our act together."

After the student laughter subsides, Mr. Spark reminds them to take their portfolios to advisories, where they will keep them and get help working on them from time to time. The first step will be to enter their current courses and get a printout from their advisory teacher that shows their attendance and other information that is already in the system for the year so far. Serious looks return to their faces as they file from the auditorium.

Mr. Spark wonders what the real impact will be. Will knowledge of the requirements and tracking their own data and progress make them more responsible? Or will the requirements look too daunting and scare some into early departure? He's not totally sure, but in his usual glass-half-full disposition, he concludes, "If it keeps even some of these kids more engaged in their education, and keeps them from closing doors on their own future, it's something we just have to do."

QUESTIONS FOR REFLECTION

1. Mr. Spark wonders whether full disclosure of the requirements and expectations will motivate students to rise to the occasion or scare them away. What is the prevailing attitude in your school? Does it need to be expressed and addressed?

2. How is faculty meeting time used in your school? Is the focus on teaching and learning, or logistics?

3. What approach is taken in your school when new external mandates are received? How do leaders convert extrinsic pressure into intrinsic motivation among students and staff?

4. As you answer these questions in your own thinking, what will you do to check the accuracy of your perceptions with students?

CONTENT FOR CONSIDERATION

Four-Year Plans

A cornerstone strategy of *Breaking Ranks II* (NASSP, 2004) is "Personalized Planning: Implement a comprehensive advisory program that ensures each student has frequent and meaningful opportunities to plan and assess his or her academic and social progress with a faculty member" (p. 6). More specifically, Recommendation 12 demands: "Each student will have a Personal Plan for Progress that will be reviewed often to ensure that the high school takes individual needs into consideration and to allow students, within reasonable parameters, to design their own methods for learning in an effort to meet high standards" (p. 18). These two statements combine to emphasize that each student is assessing his or her progress, while the school as a whole is assessing its own performance in providing options for student learning. Items in personal plans might include the following:

- Reflections on personal aspirations and an academic courses plan and school activities strategy that may lead to realization of those aspirations
- A review of personal learning styles

- Areas of strength and areas for improvement
- Specific products or portfolio items demonstrating accomplishment and progress in academic areas, school activities, sports, and school or community leadership. (pp. 10, 170–173)

At Mount Desert Island High School in Bar Harbor, Maine, students work with parents, teachers, advisers, and mentors to develop plans that include "clear goals and expectations that guide their class choices, internship or work opportunities, and career directions" (Allen, 2005, p. 4). Students are able to receive helpful feedback on the quality of their work from a range of adults, and this helps them improve their school performance and confidence. At annual conferences in September, students direct a conversation about their accomplishments and review classroom work samples and common assessments. These common assessments address key goals for learning and skill acquisition in each subject area at each grade level. In English, for example, all 9th graders critique the persuasive power of a newspaper editorial, all 10th graders analyze literature in a thesis paper, and all 11th graders complete an extensive research project. The senior year provides opportunities for more advanced course work or to retake common assessments, if necessary, to meet the graduation standard.

Senior Projects and Problems

In many districts, the senior year is devoted to a special project such as Littleton, Colorado's Senior Year Plan, which is intentionally developed to counteract the phenomenon of seniors "blowing off" their second semester. As stated in *Breaking Ranks II* (NASSP, 2004), "The focus on admission to college rather than on preparation for success in doing college-level work, the admissions calendar, and the lack of alignment between high school and college-testing programs and course work all contribute to 'checking out early' and the feeling on the part of many students that the second semester of the senior year is boring, repetitious, and pointless" (p. 116). Momentum for the senior year project begins in January of the junior year, as students conduct credit checks to verify their timeline for graduation requirements, begin a reflection piece that will carry through the senior year, and meet with their advisers. During this time, they also have assistance with applications to participate in the Postsecondary Options plan in which they can take courses for dual credit. In August of their senior year, 12th graders meet to begin organizing their second-semester plans. This includes meetings with advisers and review of grades every six weeks. By November 1, seniors submit plans that contain experiential activities or traditional course work and activities. These plans must be approved by a committee consisting of the student's parent or guardian, the student's adviser, and a community member if applicable to the specific plan. The projects and courses are completed during second semester, and small group meetings are held over several weeks in the month of May to share experiences and complete their Final Thoughts reflection piece.

For several years, the Everett, Washington, School District has incorporated a Culminating Experience for seniors. They found that the biggest challenge initially came from students' learned dependence on adults, and they had to break this ingrained pattern of students as passive, dependent learners and both convince them and teach them how to take responsibility for their own work. Everett now uses a Web-based system to help students manage their Culminating Experience, monitor their timelines, and solicit feedback. In order to provide multiple opportunities and timelines for students, Everett holds graduation ceremonies in June, August, and in the following January for students who don't get serious soon enough.

Time management issues are very real for both juniors and seniors who want to maximize their high school experience and also prepare for their future (Serrano, 2005). Classes, extracurriculars, jobs, and social life with friends compete for their hours. Counselors note that some students are tempted to join 25 clubs, play a sport in every season, and take three or more advanced placement courses in order to impress colleges. They advise students to get involved in one or two things they enjoy and commit to them for the long run. Pointers from principals and counselors to help students "take control of your schedule" include the following:

- Use a calendar or planner to note important dates, project deadlines, and social activities
- Look at all things from a year-round perspective; assign some tasks to school breaks and less stressful months, such as those between testing periods
- To avoid feeling overwhelmed, focus on the immediate task or activity before you; if you planned for a break, be in the moment of the break, not worrying about the work you will get back to
- Think before you act; make choices wisely, as they will impact all of your life

In Serrano's (2005) feature article, advice is also provided to concerned parents. "It's tempting to want to control our children's lives and step in when things don't go smoothly. Learn to step back a little, as this is the time when you're training your little ones to make those all-important decisions that can have huge effects on their lives" (p. E5). When students begin to take on too much, especially if grades drop or behavior appears to change, parents should definitely contact the school. The counselor or teacher can also observe the student more closely, and parents and the school can work together to intervene as needed.

A STUDENT GETS THE LAST WORD

Kelli Miura described her life as a senior as juggling school, extracurricular activities, a part-time job, applying for scholarships, and doing five or six hours of homework a night. To pursue her interest in journalism, she gave up her summer and winter breaks to intern for a local magazine. "At times it's been really, really stressful. It's like living in two different worlds: living in present time, but at present, you're trying to prepare for the future. . . . Whatever you have to do, don't spend time worrying about it, just do it and do it right. . . . I live by the rule 'Everything is equal to you.' This basically means whatever you do is what you get back. It's purely based on effort, so don't expect more than what you give in life" (Serrano, 2005, p. E1).

December, Year 2

Home for the Holidays

The Choir Room is full again. This time, it's the seniors and last year's graduates who are Home for the Holidays from their various postsecondary pursuits. Morris, Teri, Tom, Mike, and Gloria are all there—hoping that Joe will fill them in on what it's like at the university.

Joe enters with a different topic on his mind. He wants to know if there have been any real changes since the big assembly at the end of last year when everybody made promises to Mr. Spark. After greeting his friends, he glances around this once-familiar site of meetings and rehearsals. Amid the musical notes and choreographed steps on the board, his eyes fall on a chart that doesn't seem related to all the concerts of the season.

Five Elements of Powerful Teaching

Date of walk-throughs: October, November

No. Visits	High Expectations— clearly stated, consistently enforced	Important Content— references to standards, summarized	Student Centered— active participation, options	Challenging Material— high Bloom's, help available	Frequent Assessment— feedback from self, peers, teacher; progress noted
240	158 66%	120 50%	96 40%	72 30%	48 20%
260	178 68%	156 60%	125 48%	89 34%	57 22%

He asks Morris about it. "Well, Joe, one of the things that really is happening is that Mr. Spark is keeping the teachers focused on those elements of powerful teaching. And some of the teachers are really serious about it too. They start the lesson with telling us what we should learn and what state standards it's connected to. The ninth graders have new portfolios, and they have those state standards to refer to. Some of them are even checking to be sure their classes are getting to the ones the syllabus says they will hit. And more of my classes have an ending to them, instead of just doing your homework and waiting for the bell to ring. Teachers are reminding us of the objective, or summarizing what we did. Some of them are asking students to do the summarizing, and in those classes we really have to keep on our toes."

"That's cool. What else is going on? Mike, what's up with you?"

"Well, I got the idea that us skateboarders should get involved and build a better connection and reputation in the school, so I started up a club and got us a seat on the House of Representatives. Now we're talking to some guys at the Parks and Rec Department about where we could skateboard that wouldn't do any damage to things other people want to use."

"Wow! Mike, that is totally awesome."

"Well, that's nothing. You should see Gloria's sculptures. Mrs. Paulson helped her get some on exhibit in a gallery downtown, and a couple even got sold for holiday gifts!"

"Gloria, is that really so?! Good for you! I want to find out where that is so I can check them out. What about Teri and Tom? How's it going?"

As usual, Tom nods and Teri speaks. "After Morris and Gloria worked out some individual things with Mr. Adams and Mrs. Paulson, I decided that I should try to stick up for myself too. Mrs. Donnelly has taught me some organizational techniques and ways to help me with my reading and assignments. So I started talking to the teachers in a couple of my hard classes. I explained what I need to help me learn, and they were great. Mr. Michelson has really strict standards, and I was a little bit afraid of him, but he said he'd be glad to look over my assignment book each day and make sure I understand what I need to do. And he said that sometimes I make really good comments in class that show I understand more than he thought. So sometimes I'm going to tape-record my ideas and turn that in along with my written work, and he's going to consider both of them when he gives my grade. But Joe, now that I'm getting a handle on how I learn best, do they pay any attention to you at college about stuff like that? I'm beginning to think I could maybe go to college, but maybe it's just a reality show in my head."

"Yeah, Joe, you're supposed to be telling us what college is like. Let's get to that."

"Well, college is great except that I thought it would be great to go to a really big university, but I'm feeling a little bit lost. Fortunately, I can handle things pretty independently. But, to answer Teri's question, YES, I do think you could and should think about going to college. It's just a matter of checking out a lot of options—what kind of college, how big it is, and how much they make you take all at once. If you take less courses than some other people, but study just as many hours as they do, you can keep up, Teri. You're really serious about learning, and that's more than I can say for a lot of the freshmen at my school. They're really smart, but they're flunking out because they just aren't serious."

"Thanks, Joe. Any other advice for us?"

"Well, I'm not real sure—but I can tell you that you do need to work on the learning and the state test. My student adviser had those results when I went in to see about a schedule change. I wanted to get into a more advanced course, and he wouldn't let me take it because I was pretty loose about that test."

"Okay. We're going to be working with Mr. Spark on that right after the holidays."

"Good. Is everything else going OK?"

"Well, mostly," says Morris. "But I'm afraid the mentoring for ninth graders is falling apart a little bit. There's no time to get together with them. And now they're supposed to start with four-year plans and keep these portfolios. The teachers who have freshmen advisories are grumbling because they have to do more work than the other advisories, and they don't have time to help 20 ninth graders get their portfolios going. Mentors could help with that, but we're not around when they have their advisories."

"Have you talked to Mr. Spark about that?"

"Well, not really. He's trying to get so many things going, and there *are* changes happening, so we don't want to be complaining."

"It seems to me like he said back in May that things wouldn't work out perfectly right away, so he would want to know."

"How *much* do you think he would want to know?"

"About what? Is there something else that's not working like it should?"

"Yeah, Joe, in the middle of all the people trying real hard, there are a few teachers who just don't seem to get it. There's a couple who don't do *any* of those five things on that chart, and they seem half mad all the time. One day I was trying to be helpful, so I asked what the objective of the lesson was. Whew, I thought I was going to get one of those generic disrespectful detentions."

"Hmm. I'll bet I could predict exactly which teachers you're talking about. You know, Mr. Spark probably does want to know if that's happening. You just need to think about how to approach it. Now, what are you doing for fun the next couple of weeks?"

As Joe and the seniors from Table Ten began to mingle with the larger group, Morris began to think about the end of the semester and start of a new calendar year. Mr. Spark had mentioned that there would need to be midcourse corrections. How would students be able to voice their concerns and shape the next phase of the school's improvement efforts?

QUESTIONS FOR REFLECTION

1. What changes are students experiencing in their classes? What individual changes are they experiencing in their broader relationship with the school as a whole? Do you believe these changes are possible? Why? Why not?

2. What would teachers in your school say about who should go to college? How are those expectations conveyed in overt and subtle ways? How (and by whom) are various kinds of students assisted with postsecondary decisions and the steps needed to implement them?

3. Difficulties are arising with implementation of the advisory program and ninth-grade mentoring. What would you do next? How do you address implementation dips in your school?

4. As you answer these questions in your own thinking, what will you do to check the accuracy of your perceptions with students?

CONTENT FOR CONSIDERATION

Breaking Ranks II (NAASP, 2004) serves many schools as their road map to change. Cornerstone Strategy 4 is about "Adapting to Differences" and emphasizes the need to "[e]nsure teachers use a variety of instructional strategies and assessments to accommodate individual learning styles" (p. 6). At Knownwell High School, Morris, Gloria, and Teri have taken the initiative to work with their teachers on ways to accommodate their passions and their needs. Over a decade ago, I observed the power of students as advocates in their own learning in a small and unintentional way. Ninth-grade teachers at a high school in Oregon, Wisconsin, began implementing changes in practice that included use of the state standards and engaging students in small group activities. Perhaps they sensed that students appreciated the changes, but they didn't collect any data on their perceptions—so they were quite surprised when their students moved on and began to agitate the 10th-grade teachers. Their questions became, "Last year our teachers told us what standard we were working on. Why don't you?" "Last year our teachers let us work together. Why don't you?"

Although initially taken aback by the students' queries, 10th-grade teachers became curious enough to ask their colleagues about what they had done, and the seeds planted by the students began to take root in schoolwide growth.

This kind of student self-advocacy can indeed be disconcerting—yet it is a clear expression of the student interest and motivation teachers say they want and don't get. Only a few will take the risk of proposing changes or adjustments in their assignments and assessments. Many more would exercise options if they were offered the chance as part of their regular class procedures.

Students who are used to relying on teachers to give them total structure, direction, and information can start by being taught to say, "What can I do before I ask an adult?" Teachers may also have difficulty learning to share control of instruction. They have been taught to make the decisions in the classroom and may feel they are passing the buck and not being professionally responsible if they share control of learning with students—individually or collectively. "An emphasis on student self-direction and efficacy means that we teach and engage students in specific strategies that offer them opportunities to make decisions and solve problems on their own. . . . [W]e provide them with strategies designed to help them process information effectively and to be self-confident, believing that they have the abilities to succeed" (Barell, 1995, p. 1). In classrooms where students are self-directed, teachers engage students in setting goals and monitoring their own progress, both individually and collaboratively, in school and at home.

Foothills Academy in Calgary, Alberta, is a school of choice for students with learning problems. Its focus is on changing the self-talk of the student and then teaching students how to develop coping strategies, take control of their own learning, and return to a secondary or postsecondary education setting equipped to ensure their own success. Although it may never have been said aloud, students who come to Foothills have developed an inner language that says, "I'm dumb. I can't do it." This is modified to "I have a disability, and I am learning to work with it." Students complete checklists about their behavior and learning and then are given an inside look at what is usually "teacher only" information about the implications of their specific disability. They set goals, monitor their own progress, and participate in discussions about the rate at which they become more independent and less reliant on the available supports.

Sean, James, Alex, and Luke took time to sit and talk with me, and I asked them for an example of a time they took charge of something related to their own learning. Sean replied, "Days with substitutes were a big problem. I got in trouble when they were here, and I realized it. So I talked with my teacher about it. He said, 'Just follow along and stay cool—don't be funny with somebody who doesn't know you. I know you and appreciate your humor, but they might not because they don't know you. So you can shut it down for just one day and you won't be in trouble when I get back.' And it worked. Now sometimes I can go two whole days without getting goofy." When I told these young men that I was writing a book, Sean and James said, "Write in the book that they should help students understand their own mind. That's very important. Tell them for two reasons: so you can choose the best job for yourself in life and so you can tell teachers what you need."

Students at Foothills Academy have also had experience shaping their learning environment. When a new building was in the planning, Executive Director Gordon Bullivant created groups of students to provide input. Their suggestions and choices convey not only their preferences but some insight into their previous school experiences:

- Have the principal's office right in the middle with a window so we know he's there
- Have a smoking room at first so people don't have to stand outside in the snow—but tell staff they have to quit smoking within three years
- Have lots of windows but only with two-way glass, no one-way glass; we deserve to see who's watching us
- Put the windows low on the walls so we can see out when we need to
- Keep the walls all white so we can put work up there and it will stay clean
- Have the playground in front of the school and have the students come in the front entrance; it's our school and people going by should know it's a place where children are; the staff can park in the back
- Put "WELCOME" on the door instead of "Go to the office"
- Have more bathrooms with less toilets in each one so the younger kids won't be frightened to go in and the bigger kids won't fool around too long

An interesting footnote is Bullivant's observation that almost all students from Foothills go on to postsecondary education, and many become special education teachers.

A STUDENT GETS THE LAST WORD

Luke was a "jittery" young man who had little to say during most of my group conversation with his pals. Then I asked each one individually about the school, and Luke offered, "Teachers are better here." When I probed for what a good teacher is and how these are better, he started, "They're friendly with you . . ." and then seemed to choke up and walked away. I was sad to see him go, and finished the interview. Five minutes later, I noticed Luke watching from his classroom door as I gathered up my things. He approached me alone and said in halting phrases, "There is something I want to say about teachers. It's more than friendly. They actually *teach* me. I don't know how to explain what they do that's so different, but I can tell it's different—because I'm *getting* it."

17

January, Year 2

Progress Checks

The midyear staff development day is coming up. As he did last year, Mr. Spark has issued an invitation to interested students. During the first part of the day, participants will meet in the same configuration of study groups: Three R's focused on learning and essential skills, plus the other two R's of Relationships and Responsibility. The purpose of the morning session will be to review the strategies that were chosen and identify evidence that shows progress toward implementation and impact. The guiding questions for the conversations are simple:

- Are we working our plan?
- Is our plan working to meet our goals?

Teri and Tom are among the students meeting with Miss Pope, Mrs. Donnelly, and other teachers of the Three R's study group. They have the third round of data from Mr. Spark's walk-through chart as one source of evidence to review.

Five Elements of Powerful Teaching

Date of walk-throughs: October, November, December

No. Visits	High Expectations— clearly stated, consistently enforced	Important Content— references to standards, summarized	Student Centered— active participation, options	Challenging Material— high Bloom's, help available	Frequent Assessment— feedback from self, peers, teacher; progress noted
240	158 66%	120 50%	96 40%	72 30%	48 20%
260	178 68%	156 60%	125 48%	89 34%	57 22%
225	175 78%	167 74%	140 62%	101 45%	81 36%

"They didn't get to classrooms as many times in December, did they?" observes Tom. Always his counterpoint, Teri adds, "Well, that's understandable with almost two weeks of the month shut down for the holidays. So let's just look at the percentages and not the number of times they noticed things."

"OK. The percentages are higher in all five elements. That's good news. And most of my friends have been saying that it's getting more interesting in class."

"Right. But the same two things are still the lowest: challenging material and frequent assessment. Miss Pope, are those two the hardest for teachers to do?"

"Well, speaking just for myself, I can tell you a couple of things about my training as a teacher. I was taught that challenging material would be reserved for my Honors courses because it would be too complicated for most students. And in student teaching, I never saw any kind of assessment except midterm and final exams. So it's just not something I've had on my radar screen. Let's capture that question here for further discussion after we look at some other evidence."

Other teachers in the room nodded, and one ventured a second question. "Except for the teachers on formal evaluation, the administrators can only be in our classrooms for quick walk-throughs. Maybe there's more progress than they can see in those short visits. Would there be a way to get more information or another viewpoint?"

Mrs. Donnelly responds. "Well, you know who *is* in the classroom for every lesson, don't you?"

Students chuckle at the puzzled looks prompted by her question and chime in helpfully. "She's talking about us—we're there the whole time. And believe me, we know whether those five things are happening or not."

Another teacher reminds the group that a student survey was very useful the previous spring and suggests that the idea of student feedback be added to the list of topics for further discussion.

Miss Pope then asks about the other strategies that had been identified to impact learning of essential skills, or the three R's, as they were dubbed. "We flexed some schedules so there could be morning and afternoon skinny periods for students to get help. What evidence do we have about our progress there?"

Mr. Michelson speaks up. "I have to say that I only volunteered to do the morning skinny period because I get here early anyway, and I figured there wouldn't be any students and it wouldn't really change anything. But I have had anywhere from two to eight students almost every day, and they are coming with specific questions that I can usually help them with rather quickly. I really didn't think that students cared that much about their learning. I guess they rise to the occasion when there's a way to get past something they're stuck on."

Teri adds, "Having it in each department really helps too. Then you're not trying to get math help from a social studies teacher who . . . uh . . . well, doesn't have that as a major."

Amid chuckles, another teacher comments. "I've had kids in after school too. They say it makes a huge difference when they have a choice of morning or afternoon that will fit their schedules. I looked at the appointment book one of them was using, and I guess I had forgotten how crammed their time is."

"Yeah, this has been kind of like one of those *Field of Dreams* things."

Amid a chorus of "huh's?" and "what's?" he continues. "You know, 'Build it and they will come.'"

"Oh, right."

"Yeah, that's good."

Teri speaks up again. "I'm one student who uses the help period a lot. But I sort of wonder if it's a pain to the teachers. Like, Mr. Michelson, does it bug you that we really come and you don't have the time to yourself?"

"Well, I did discover that if something is really due the next day, I need to make sure it's done the night before in case I have lots of students for help time. But I sure wouldn't call it a pain. It's actually a nice way to start the day—with kids that are interested and motivated to get there that early. Don't worry—it's worth it."

Miss Pope focuses the group again. "We also had that inservice in August on thinking strategies to help with reading comprehension. How's that going?"

A long pause ensues. Once more, it's Teri who breaks the silence. "At the beginning of the year, quite a few of my teachers went through the textbook to show us how to start reading a chapter. That was cool."

Tom chimes in. "One of my teachers started talking about how she thinks in her head when she's reading things. Like, she reads to us for a little bit, and then she lays down the book and says things like 'I'm wondering what is going to happen next' or 'I think this fits with something I heard on the news.' Did that come from your inservice?"

"Yes, it did. So did some other things like visualizing and using organizers and fix-up strategies for when you get stuck."

"Really? Fix-up strategies? Where can I learn about that?"

"Well, I guess that's another area for further discussion. We were hoping we could weave that into our regular classes, but maybe we need another approach."

Teri persists. "Yes, that should be in our regular classes. But I can tell from that chart we looked at that it takes a while to get new things going in our regular classes. I think we should have a Power Reading class right away if there are things I can do to help read faster or understand it better."

"You're right. We talked about a Power Reading class last spring, and we need to get on with it. Now, we have evidence that the five elements of powerful teaching are being implemented, and we have evidence that the morning and afternoon skinny periods are used by students. We also have questions about implementation of the thinking strategies for reading. Our other guiding question is whether we can see the impact of these changes. Can we tell if students *are* learning more or doing better in other ways?"

"We might need another month to answer that. We'll have the D/F lists from first semester. I know that my list is the shortest it's ever been." Other teachers nod in agreement.

"Yes, we should look at that and also at overall GPAs. We should be able to see some changes there."

"Right. And the reality is—we also have to get back to talking about the state test pretty soon. Because that's one of the bottom-line measures. Will we be able to see those results improve as a result of our school improvement strategies?"

Meanwhile, Morris and Gloria are meeting with the Relationships group. Along with Mrs. Halverson, they are explaining that they've run into a snag with the mentoring program for ninth graders. They are getting e-mails from some of their mentees who wanted to get together, but there doesn't seem to be any time built in for it to happen. Each grade level is on a different lunch period, so they can't get together then. They might try to meet before or after school, but that competes with going to the help sessions that they also seem to need.

"OK, so we need to brainstorm some ways for ninth graders and mentors to be able to interact throughout the year, not just at the start of school. Is that what you're saying, Morris?"

"Yes, thanks. We might not be able to change this year, but I think we need to come up with something for next year for sure."

Mrs. Halverson moves the discussion on to the topic of advisories. "This year we added 10 more minutes to the short period that used to be homerooms. How's that going?"

Murmurs emerge from around the room. Finally, Mr. Shepley speaks his mind. "I'll be honest. I don't get what I'm supposed to do with this group of kids. They're not in my classes, so I don't really know them. And I got stuck with ninth graders, so now they're telling me that I'm supposed to help them with these four-year plans and what to put in their portfolios. Maybe we jumped into that too fast. I just dread my advisory. I mean, sorry, Morris, but this just isn't working for me."

"Well, the point is for us to be honest here, so that's OK. Because I can tell you, some of the advisories aren't working very well from the students' point of view either. Some teachers just treat it like a study hall—take your books out and do homework. So the idea that it's for relationships is a crock. Remember that survey you didn't like—where kids said they didn't have anybody they knew well in the school that they could talk to? Well, we were hoping that advisories would be the place where some relationships would get established."

Gloria joins in. "You say that you don't know the kids. Well, what are you doing to get to know them? How do you get to know adults that you meet? Do you ask them about themselves? You don't have to know what we want to do or talk about—just *ask* us."

"Well, you have a point. Maybe I've been trying to make it too complicated. But some of us want activities to use or some material to follow. So I want to talk more later today about lessons for advisories." Mrs. Halverson and the students exchange worried looks as Mr. Ralston lists the topic on the whiteboard.

"A third thing that we implemented this year is the realignment of counselors by the alphabet instead of by grade. It's easy to answer the first question about whether we're doing the plan—because it was a very clear structural change. Do we have any observations about whether it's having an impact on relationships?"

A student who's been slumped in a chair in the back row leans forward. "Well, I can tell you that it's had an impact on my family. Now that all three of us kids have the same counselor, she's calling my mom every couple of weeks and telling them how much better we're doing—at least two out of three of us are—and giving suggestions and stuff. She said it's like having fewer students because they're more connected. I gotta say—I used to wish somebody would pay more attention, but it could be turning out as too much of a good thing."

As laughter unites students and teachers, Mrs. Halverson is glad to have this part of the day come to an end. It's clear that there are implementation challenges with the mentor program and advisories, and she's not sure the solutions in teachers' minds are going to play out well with the students. She wonders how she will facilitate the afternoon discussion. "What if I have to compromise the true intent in order to keep from losing the whole thing?"

The mood is more positive as Mr. O'Brien and Mr. Soderberg facilitate the Responsibility group. Mike has just presented a list of the groups that are now represented in the House of Representatives. By adding up the number of students in those groups, he has presented quantitative evidence of more students emerging as active participants in student leadership. He has also shared anecdotal evidence of students he knows that planned to drop out but so far are still hanging in. He blushes at the unexpected round of applause he receives from the group.

Mr. O'Brien summarizes. "So, one of our strategies has some clear answers to the questions of whether we are doing it and if it's having an impact. Another thing we were concerned about were the discipline referrals happening to ninth graders at the start of the year. So we worked on one set of common rules to help with consistency among teachers and clarity among students. Mr. Soderberg has some evidence to share with us on that topic."

The evidence is a graph of discipline referrals for the first four months of this year compared with the two previous years. The green bars for this year are dramatically lower than the black and gray bars showing the past. Participants nod and smile at the evidence of impact from this move toward common expectations.

Mr. O'Brien then steers discussion toward the topic of four-year plans and portfolios. "We really wanted to learn how this could work, and it seems like the best way to get students to take responsibility for their school experience. But we've only had a couple of months to work with this, and December's a short one—so our discussion is very preliminary and probably premature for making any changes. But what's your take on it so far?"

"Well, I think the concept is great. But I'm hearing from some of my colleagues that putting it on advisory teachers is unfair because only one-fourth of the teachers are stuck with all the work. And they're not sure what they should be doing, and neither are the students. And the mentors are supposed to be helping the ninth graders, but they aren't getting together on it."

Mr. Spark has been roving among the various groups and enters just in time to hear the last few comments. He recalls hearing about the advisories in some other sessions as well. "Déjà vu all over again," he thinks, as he realizes that implementing advisories seemed like just adding more minutes to that period. "I felt so good about that one. Guess I really underestimated the implementation challenges. I wonder what will happen next. And I hope I don't have to referee between two groups who have different thoughts about what we should do."

QUESTIONS FOR REFLECTION

1. Mr. Michelson has changed his thinking and his own time management. In what ways? Why and how did that happen? Could it happen in your school? Should it?

2. What changes in good assessment practices have occurred since teachers in your school received their training? When they answer, "What were you teaching today?" can they also answer, "Which students learned it and how do you know?"

3. What should Mr. Spark do about the aversion to advisories that he is hearing?

4. List the strategies that are identified in your current school improvement plans. What evidence are you gathering so you will be able to answer the questions of "Are we working our plan?" and "Is our plan working to meet our goals?" (Holcomb, 2004).

5. As you answer these questions in your own thinking, what will you do to check the accuracy of your perceptions with students?

CONTENT FOR CONSIDERATION

Advisory programs come highly recommended in *Breaking Ranks II* (NAASP, 2004) and many other sources of research and advocacy about high school reform. They also come fraught with factors that affect successful implementation. Many schools will say they have "tried advisories" and they didn't work. "Often these have been little more than 'homeroom,' opportunities to distribute paperwork, or time for school announcements" (p. 10).

At Squalicum High School in Bellingham, Washington, the first attempt at an advisory program was evaluated after less than one year of implementation. Students were asked if it was valuable, and 70 percent replied that they wanted to keep having advisories. Staff were given an opportunity to vote, and even with this strong expression of student voice, 80 percent voted to discontinue the practice. Part of the problem was lack of clear answers to typical implementation questions (Holcomb, 2004): "What will it look like? Sound like? What will teachers be doing? What will students be doing? What evidence will be present in the classroom? Who will notice the change? What do we hope they will say?" If people don't have a clear and shared image of what's intended, everyone has a different set of expectations and few will be satisfied with what they see.

Advisories also ran into trouble at Kittitas High School in Washington State (Lambert, 2003). Implemented in the fall of 2002, each group had 12 or 13 students and met for half an hour each week. A major goal was to provide each student with a close connection to an adult. "However, when we listened to the kids, we learned we weren't meeting that goal," acknowledged Principal Doug Maynard. "In January, we gathered together two student representatives from each advisory and asked for their opinions. What we heard was that while advisories were useful for making connections to other students, they weren't helping kids make that connection with an adult" (p. 1).

As their next step, they decided to take students to see successful advisory programs at other schools. Doug and the students put together a list of questions to use during the trip. At Vancouver (Washington) School of the Arts and at Merlo Station in Beaverton, Oregon, they sat in advisories, interviewed students, and filled notebooks with their observations. Student Michelle Krueger really liked what she saw at Merlo Station. "Students were totally open with their advisors and we heard a lot about how kids would go to them with their problems. I thought that one of the reasons it worked so well was because students spend so much time with their advisors" (Lambert, 2003, pp. 1–2). At Merlo Station, advisories met daily, not weekly, for 100 minutes—75 minutes for connective and goal-setting activities and 25 minutes for academic work. As Michelle summed it up, "I learned that advisories *can* work and that they can help build great relationships with teachers. . . . Our advisories need to meet more often" (p. 2).

Relationships between adults and students are also highly prized at Calgary (Alberta) Alternative High School (AHS), one of the few schools remaining after the 1970s rise and fall of alternative schools. Students must apply to attend, must adhere strictly to the zero-tolerance policy regarding substances, and must actively participate in their learning and in their schoolwide DGM's (Democratic General Meetings). In addition, students volunteer for many roles within the school, including voluntary attendance on recent professional development days to work with staff on revising the school's Vision and Mission Statement.

Each teacher serves as mentor for the progress of about 12 students, and students have the freedom to influence course content and the method in which they learn. Most instruction is conducted in small groups and tutorials, and students are encouraged to develop learning strategies that will promote their best learning and work on personal projects.

Principal John Fischer described a recent survey conducted in the high schools of Area IV in Calgary who were studying personalization and student engagement. Summarizing the data from AHS, he commented in his newsletter: "This data reflects the emphasis we put on building a community and honoring student voice" (Calgary Board of Education, 2005, p. 1).

- Students said that mentors know them personally. Many suggested that all the staff members knew them and they could go to other teachers for help. This was at a personal level.
- Students cited discussion and being self-directed as the type of studying they like to do. They felt that being pushed to their full potential is important. Others described the flexible, negotiable, project work that

teachers tailor to suit the students. One group mentioned that "busy work," such as worksheets and questions, doesn't work for them.

- Students agreed that the school is set up so that everyone can be successful, but their responses underscore the onus on each student. The Step System is offered as the way that the school supports this.
- Teaching what has been learned to others was mentioned several times as a way to deepen learning. Specifically, students mentioned weekly goal setting and the sheets used for tracking and the Step System. They said they developed good understanding when there is consistent feedback and there is time to learn.
- Small classes and chances to work with teachers was the most important factor that works for students as learners. Learning in a positive environment where they could find a place to focus was important. Again, challenging learning activities were mentioned. What didn't work was a place where there were too many distractions.
- Students agreed that AHS helps to develop their character. They said that they work without rules and that working with agreements promotes their independence. They also described how AHS teaches responsibility and how this works in relationship to academic honesty. They mentioned how important freedom is and how this connects to their "sense of self."
- Students supported the statement that "our school respects people's needs to take responsibility and to give back to the community." They gave several examples of processes in AHS that support this. Democratic Living and Learning challenges, recycling, campout, and DGM were cited.

This survey highlights how students feel about the school and how well connected they are to AHS. It provides some data that support how we feel about teaching and learning and how excited we are about the successes and achievement of the students (Calgary Board of Education, 2005).

My conversations with Amanda, Kurt, Gerald, Andrew, and Paul at AHS were fascinating. When asked to compare AHS with their previous schools, they weren't shy in their criticism:

- Students all split off into groups there. If you didn't have a group, you're a nobody.
- The atmosphere is different here. Students and teachers are the same group; there's more communication and community.
- The staff at the other school are uneducated about people and their problems. They're apathetic to the problems of students. Instead they just brought in "feel good" presentations as a way of being antidrug and antiviolence.

- Other schools have a "fill in the blanks" mentality. Here there's more real thinking, even debating in classes. The curriculum in regular schools is just facts.
- You can fly under the radar there—here you can only hide for about 10 minutes.

These students don't just identify problems, though. They had strong recommendations for schools who want to keep their students:

- One key is overcoming the teachers' authoritative complex. They come across so strong as the be-all and know-all that it just makes you *want* to rebel.
- They might think of using a first-name basis.
- They treat students like tools—so if they treat people that way, all you get is just obedience, not respect. Students and teachers should have mutual respect.
- Another thing that should happen is to break down cliques—get all people involved in group initiatives so everyone can be part of the whole.
- It's partly what not to do. Forget the canned programs that are supposed to help self-esteem. They're all talk and no action. You can't teach it; you have to model it. They have to show honest respect, not phony "techniques."
- Some of the seminars they have about bullying—they're useless. They just developed them to keep from getting sued. If they really cared, they would be paying attention.

A STUDENT GETS THE LAST WORD

Deborah, a graduating senior in Ohio, talked about paying attention to students and students observing teaching:

Go to the kids more for evaluation because we're the ones who sit there every day. . . . [W]e could give an honest opinion. . . . [A]sk the whole class and you could get a fair opinion. It is still important for administrators to observe, but ask the people who have been observing *all year long!* (Platt et al., 2000, p. 196)

18

February, Year 2

Midcourse Corrections and Congratulations

"**M**r. Spark, Mr. Spark," Morris is completely out of character. His usual shuffle is replaced by a mad dash across the Commons to catch up with his principal. Half out of breath, he skips any greeting and his customary request for permission to share an idea or concern. "Mr. Spark, what did you let them do to advisories?!"

"Oh, Morris. I was afraid you were going to be disappointed. I've been trying for the last couple of days to hook up with you about this, but I've had extra meetings to attend outside the school and just didn't get it done. Is it the ninth-grade advisories that you're upset about? I know you have a lot invested in the mentoring program, and I can assure you we're not trying to replace or decrease the importance of the student-to-student support and peer relationships."

"No, Mr. Spark, that's not it. I know the teachers haven't really gotten their arms around the four-year plans and portfolios, and if the administrators and counselors are teaming up with them to go into the ninth-grade advisories every other day and help them get this going—that's great. I mean, that's more work for you, but I know the teachers with ninth-grade advisories were complaining and I want to be sure the ninth graders do get the help, and there doesn't seem to be time for mentors to get together with them on that. So that's OK with the ninth graders. But this stuff they're doing in the other grade advisories is stupid. Sorry."

"I guess you're referring to the character education activities that some people are piloting, right?"

"What does 'piloting' mean? Does it mean an experiment?"

"That's fairly accurate, Morris. It means that some teachers are using this material they wanted to try, but not every teacher is doing it, and it will be re-evaluated in a while."

"Why did you let them even do that? It's such phony stuff. It's not what advisories were supposed to be."

"I know, Morris. And I'm not thrilled about it. But there were some strong feelings and suggestions to drop the whole idea of advisories and just have the old style homeroom for announcements and study hall. I had a whole bunch of short talks with Mrs. Halverson and the group on inservice day and then with the administrators and the department heads. Even though I hated to, it seemed like if there wasn't some help put into ninth-grade advisories, and some compromises about the other grades, there might get to be more and more of a push to stop having advisories altogether."

"Well, having advisories is important for *both* relationships and responsibility, so I guess if that's the only way you could hang onto them . . . I mean, you're the man, you have to decide. But *who* is going to re-evaluate them? Over at the other school, they tried advisories and had trouble with them, so they voted. A big majority of the students wanted them, but most of the teachers didn't—and they just ignored what the students said and dropped them. If kids think their voice is going to be ignored, everything we've been doing for student involvement is right down the—uh—toilet."

"Well, we won't be putting anything as important as that to a simple vote, Morris. We'll be talking about it and getting lots of viewpoints and trying to make a decision through discussion, not voting. We might have to change the whole approach to advisories for next year in order to give it a better chance."

"Well, I'm glad the ninth-grade advisories will work better. Maybe you and the counselors can show people how it ought to be, and that might change their minds. Don't give up on it, Mr. Spark—promise."

"You have my promise, Morris. I want a true advisory program to be part of our school." As Morris settles into his usual shuffle off to class, Mr. Spark rubs his neck and wonders, "I'm pushing change about as hard as I can. How am I going to deliver on that promise?"

"Miss Pope. Miss Pope." Teri spots one of her heroes in the hall and weaves her way between bodies like a salmon struggling upstream to catch up with her. "Miss Pope. That survey we did in class today was really cool. It really gave us a way to think about what's going on in our classes. You did a good job getting the teachers to go along with it. Was it hard to get that put together?"

Figure 18.1   Student Perceptions of Learning Experiences

Please take a few minutes to complete this survey. The information will help us review our progress and identify areas for further support and staff development.
These questions are about **the class that just ended**:

	Yes	No
Did the teacher share the learning goals for the class with you?		
Was there a summary of ideas at the end of the period?		
Did you have opportunities for active participation?		
Did the material challenge you to think deeply?		
Do you know how to get help if you need it with this lesson?		
Did you receive feedback on your work from teacher, peer, or self-evaluation?		
Do you know your status and progress so far in this class?		

Please think back over **your last five class periods,** including yesterday if necessary.
Check the number of classes in which each of these activities took place.

	5	4	3	2	1
I listened to the teacher talk/lecture and took notes.					
I was given a reading assignment.					
The teacher gave me ideas about how to approach my reading.					
I worked independently on a short- or long-term research-based project.					
I answered questions on a worksheet or from a textbook.					
I participated in a class discussion.					
I worked on an assignment with a small group of students.					
I worked independently on a daily assignment.					
I watched another student or small group give a performance or participated in one myself.					
I did lab work or learned by experimenting with an idea.					
I was given free time.					
I was off task and not doing what the teacher expected me to do.					
I had a chance to shape my assignment or propose a project.					

Please think about **your classes in general** and comment on any changes you observe in your learning experiences.

Thank you for your input.

"No, Teri, it wasn't as hard as it would have been a year or two ago. After the morning discussion on inservice day, we put it together pretty quickly, because we just matched up with the five elements of powerful teaching and some of the ways of engaging students that we had studied about. The hard part might be coming up next. We have to discuss the results and what to do about them. Each department collected their own at the end of that day, and they're talking about them in department meetings. They'll report out at the next faculty meeting—summarizing their observations and outlining what they think needs to happen next. Teachers are really used to working as departments, and we felt we had to give them that comfortable setting, since some of them were uneasy about this feedback from students."

"Well, I'm sure curious about whether our survey input will be anything like what Mr. Spark and the administrators have put in the charts from their visits. By the way, does Mr. Spark only evaluate certain teachers each year, or can he evaluate anybody?"

"There's a schedule of when teachers have formal evaluation. But that's a minimum. Mr. Spark can work with any teacher if there's a need for it."

"Oh . . . then . . . well, thanks, Miss Pope."

Classes fall silent as Mr. Spark requests attention for an important announcement. "Ladies and gentlemen—and I mean young ladies and gentlemen of the student body—*and* the ladies and gentlemen of the teaching and support staff. I interrupt you today to congratulate you on some information I have compiled in the last couple of weeks. The 'powerful teaching' work that teachers have been doing and the Collective Commitments that students have been practicing are paying off big time. Here's what I've discovered about first semester:

- Attendance is better than it has been in the past four years. Congratulations! Thanks for showing up!
- Discipline referrals are down—especially among ninth graders! Congratulations on the most successful entry to high school ever!

"These data provide evidence of our mutual work on respect, relationships, and responsibility. And then there's the three R's, as we call our work on essential learning. I am delighted to report that

- I have never seen such short D/F lists in all my time as a principal or assistant principal.

- And, finally, the average of GPAs for every grade level has improved from first semester of the last four years—and is especially high for the ninth graders!

"Congratulations to teachers, mentors, and students for your great effort and this proof of your success! If you are as proud of yourselves as I am proud of you, let me hear it all the way down here to the office!"

When Mr. Spark asks for silence, he always gets it. And when he asks for noise, he gets that too. The cheers echo through the hallways and reverberate all the way back to the office, resonating in the heart of the principal.

QUESTIONS FOR REFLECTION

1. Mr. Spark struck a compromise to keep advisories alive. What was it? Is compromise a bad thing? Why? Why not? What would you have done in your school?

2. For the first time, students were responding to a survey about specific teaching practices. How was it handled to increase the comfort level of staff members? What other suggestions do you have?

3. How do you use evidence of implementation and impact to celebrate progress? What rituals, traditions, and celebrations of your school culture reinforce effort and risk taking on the part of staff and students?

4. As you answer these questions in your own thinking, what will you do to check the accuracy of your perceptions with students?

CONTENT FOR CONSIDERATION

Becky Elmendorf, principal of Squalicum High School in Bellingham, Washington, was on her way down the hallway carrying a tablet and pen. One of her students approached her and asked, "Mrs. Elmendorf, are you going on a classroom observation?" When she answered yes and identified her destination, the student responded. "You don't need to go there, she's great. You really ought to be doing an observation in [Room X] instead. 'Scuse me for saying so, but it's pretty bad and the kids are suffering for it."

Student feedback on teaching and learning experiences can take a variety of forms and can provide opportunities for students of any age. At the youngest and simplest end of the continuum, a half sheet of paper can contain simple sentences like

- I understood this lesson.
- I can do this kind of work by myself.
- I could take what I learned today and use it in real life.
- I need some more help with. . . .

Responses can be a choice of icons with facial expressions ranging from excited to puzzled to frustrated, or numerical responses for levels of agreement to disagreement.

A survey like the one used at Knownwell High School is more sophisticated and specific but doesn't come close to the level of feedback provided at George Mitchell School in East London. Pupils here have been given ownership of their schooling and take it very seriously. They observe and critique lessons, make suggestions to teachers about how they could teach better, and interview candidates for teaching posts. Head teacher Helen Jeffery says, "There is a lot of lip service given to the idea of student involvement in education, but I had never seen pupils given an honest say. We wanted our students to have this. And the feedback we've had from them has been amazing. My experience with children told me they would rise to the occasion and there has not been one single instance where children have behaved maliciously or malevolently" (Wilce, 2006, p. 1). As part of the Making Learning Better program, students participate in the selection of teachers for the school. A 13-year-old student noted that "when we helped appoint a teacher we looked for someone who was strict but fair. We watched them teach a lesson. Some of them were too strict and old-fashioned, and some of them couldn't control the class properly." Some teachers were uncomfortable with the increasing role of students, and a few left. Meanwhile, other schools invited the student observers to visit their schools, contribute to inservice teacher training, and attend curriculum meetings about grouping practices. Assistant head teacher Savage reported that "[i]n meetings, they are a lot better behaved than the teachers." Although the school remains low on the charts of achievement, it was among the top 100 schools in the country for percentage improvement, moving from 20 percent of students successful in 2002 to 43 percent in 2004.

In this country, the most intense end of the continuum of student feedback may be the Best Practices Club at Lexington High School in Lexington, Massachusetts. These students recognized that a lot of student talk may be negative, but "students also can pinpoint exactly what is wrong with a particular teaching method within minutes of leaving the classroom. Likewise, there are plenty of students who know what *is* working for them, and they can explain exactly why" (Rothstein, 2006, p. 32). But there was no formal place for students to share their insights, so

10 students decided to create a forum. They began by keeping their messages positive, highlighting what was working, and hoped that teachers and administrators would respect, listen to, and learn from them. Eight "brave pioneers" agreed to be observed by the students and participate in the first student-teacher discussion on effective teaching methods. Based on this success, students requested a special facultywide workshop hosted by students. In five classrooms, pairs of student presenters started the sessions and engaged teachers in discussion. A few expressed mild irritation, but the vast majority reacted positively, and 75 of 150 indicated they would be willing to have students come into their classrooms.

A STUDENT GETS THE LAST WORD

Student author Ariela Rothstein (2006) writes,

> I would love for more students, teachers, and administrators to find their own way to incorporate a Best Practices-type club into their schools. Here are some things that can be done immediately:
>
> - Create a joint faculty-student panel on improving teaching and learning at your school.
> - Use our observation tool or create your own for students to gather information about best practices.
> - Find opportunities for students and teachers to discuss how to improve the learning community at your school. (p. 33)

March, Year 2

Advisory Adversity and Failure to Meet Commitments

The Choir Room is full again for this important faculty meeting. The atmosphere is quiet, expectant, a little nervous. Several groups have updates to provide and recommendations to consider. After celebrating progress from the first semester, it's already time to be thinking ahead to next year.

The Three R's report on powerful teaching and learning essential skills comes first. Miss Pope sets the stage with a review of the data that Mr. Spark and the administrators have been collecting during their classroom walk-throughs and the discussion that led to the student survey about their learning experiences. Each department chair is then given a few minutes to comment on the survey results. Although the adults expected some differences by departments, students were quite consistent. To Mr. Spark's relief, the survey mirrored the walk-through classroom observation data: Just not enough challenging material and very little formative assessment and feedback. Finally one teacher voices the question Mr. Spark was pondering, "How can we expect them to show responsibility for their own learning in the absence of feedback about their performance and progress?"

Another teacher adds, "And how can we motivate them if they don't find the material challenging and relevant?"

"It's a strange thing I'm noticing," says another. "I used to think it was the low performers who weren't motivated. But since we started the department help periods, I've seen that they *do* want to learn and they put forth a lot of effort when they have hope that it will pay off. What I'm noticing now is that the top students don't really put forth their best. It's like they're thinking—'What's the least I can do and still manage to keep the A grade?' But when they see something as really important to them, or to the world, they crank it up a little more. So we do have to take this seriously."

Miss Pope asks for their recommendations for next steps. "Does anyone disagree with the need for us to improve in these areas?" No argument is raised. "Is this something we need as a focus for more professional development next year? Should we look for a consultant who specializes in these aspects of teaching?" Sidebar conversations occur in low voices between twos and threes around the room. Miss Pope calls on the group to share with all, thinking, "They're just like my kids."

"Well, according to the students, some teachers are doing a great job of making classes relevant and engaging. I'm not sure we need a consultant. We might be better off to learn from each other. There's time when we do department work that really wouldn't have to take so long. And there are groups of us with common planning times when we are supposed to be doing planning together. We could focus that time on specifically helping each other add challenging material and critical thinking and formative assessment to our unit and lesson plans. I'm not sure quite how that sort of teamwork would look, but I think we have great resources right here in the school that we should tap."

"Will it seem like some teachers are better than others then? We've always tried to have a collegial culture, and it might look like we're putting some above others."

"I used to think that way. And it does make me a little nervous to think about admitting I'm not sure how to take my teaching to the next level. But instead of thinking *we're* all equal, we should be thinking about giving all of our students *equally good* learning experiences. So I'll take the lead and say that I want to learn more and I want to learn from somebody right here who works with the same students I do."

"Okay, here's a thought. Instead of another consultant to do more workshops on powerful teaching, what if we have a consultant to teach us how to discuss lessons together?"

The Choir Room is an appropriate setting for the chorus of approval that follows. Miss Pope summarizes, "So . . . we accept the data from students and administrators that we need to improve the use of challenging material, higher-level thinking, and frequent assessment with feedback. And . . . to improve in that area, we will learn some protocols for reviewing lessons together and make a commitment to designate certain common planning times for that purpose. Give me a thumbs-up if that's our consensus. Anyone with grave reservations that would keep you from participating and supporting your peers' participation? Great. I'm so proud to be part of a faculty that's not just collegial in the way we get along together but willing to affirm special strengths among us and learn from each other."

Miss Pope turns to Mr. Spark to continue with the next recommendation. "Some of you have been incorporating the thinking strategies for reading comprehension into your classes—enough so that students are aware of them, but not enough for it to show up as a common practice in the student survey results. We've heard individual comments from a number of students that they would like a more intense dose. They've suggested a separate class as an elective, something like Reading Power, so it's more like an enrichment class than a remedial class. Even some pretty good students have said they'd like to improve their reading before they go to college. Miss Pope has agreed to teach it, but as we've looked at the schedule, we can't find a way to do it without having an impact overall. We would have to cut one section of English and increase class sizes by two or three kids in order to make it work. We think we can assure you that no section would be more than 26 or 27. And of course, we think improvement of students' reading skills will benefit everyone. What are your thoughts?"

After some discussion, the faculty supports further work on the schedule to see how a Reading Power class can be included. Mr. Spark clarifies, "Now—if we do have a specific class with intense, explicit teaching of cognitive strategies for reading comprehension, how many of you think that lets you out of the expectation that you include these strategies in your own classes?" Sheepish glances here and there, a lifted eyebrow or two, some sighs, but no disagreement. Mr. Spark declares a 90-second stretch-in-place break as Mr. O'Brien and Mrs. Halverson prepare to tackle the next topic.

Mr. Spark begins. "We've made real progress this year. I'm very proud and want to remind you of the key points from our first semester data:

- Best attendance in the past four years!
- Discipline referrals are down—especially among ninth graders!
- Shortest D/F lists I've ever seen!
- GPAs for every grade level highest of last four years—and especially for our ninth graders!

So, we're doing a whole lot of things right and making a lot of changes with very few downsides. But . . . we have one area where we're getting stuck, and that's with advisories. That's a concern from both the perspective of relationships and responsibility, so Mr. O'Brien and Mrs. Halverson are doing this next section together. They will provide you with some perspectives and recommendations that might be the biggest changes we've made yet. I want you to have time to think seriously about them, so we won't be making decisions today. I also want you to know where I stand. We can explore a lot of options, but going back to traditional homerooms is not one of them. Setting aside a period for announcements and homework—where kids are passive, teachers are doing e-mail, and there's no interaction—that is too far out of sync with our Mission to be acceptable. Mr. O'Brien."

As Mr. O'Brien steps forward, he's thankful for a principal who wants and values input and participation in decision making—from *both* staff and students—but is also willing to take a stand and identify some nonnegotiables.

"Our work on responsibility has focused on two aspects of the Mission Statement: producing high quality work and practicing responsible citizenship. We've interpreted citizenship as including participation in democracy, so we made changes in student government that have engaged a lot more students in leadership roles. We've also interpreted citizenship to mean constructive or 'law-abiding' behavior and worked with students on the Collective Commitments and with you on the common classroom rules to help our ninth graders. But we got a slower start in the area of responsibility for their learning and for producing high quality work. When we heard about the state requirement for four-year plans and portfolios, it seemed like something we could start a year early and get the jump on, plus use as a focus for tracking their progress. It needed to have a place, and we put it in advisories. We still think that's a logical spot for it, and we will have to start with it next year anyway, but we did overlook a couple of things and we have to do a mea culpa here. We didn't give enough guidance to advisory teachers about how it would look or what to tell students, and worse yet, I don't know why it didn't dawn on us that the way we have advisories assigned puts all the ninth graders in certain advisories, so it put all of this on a certain group of teachers. Sorry about that. Believe me, we've heard about it, and we accept responsibility."

"Yeah, you're the Responsibility group. You *should* accept responsibility." The tongue-in-cheek rejoinder is like a pressure valve relieving the tension in the room.

Mrs. Halverson follows. "So, we have one group seeing advisories as the avenue to responsibility. Whether they did it just right or not is beside the point at the moment. Those of us focused on relationships were aiming toward that Mission phrase about 'mutually respectful environment.' We believed, and still do believe, that mutual respect can be practiced through collective commitments and common rules and expectations—but that we want it to be more authentic and intrinsic than that. We believe that genuine mutual respect comes from knowing the other well enough to appreciate strengths and also care about helping with struggles. We saw advisories as the place where we could build that kind of relationship.

"Some of our other efforts worked well. The realignment of counselors by alphabet rather than grade level is helping us be more focused, and we are getting a lot of favorable responses from parents. And our mentoring program to hook up seniors and ninth graders worked well in August. But what we overlooked was the issue of where and when ninth graders and their mentors could get together on an ongoing basis through the year. We didn't provide that, and we've heard about it from ninth graders and from seniors. And the only place or time we can figure out is, you guessed it, advisory time."

"So, here we are. We have ninth-grade advisories overloaded with the new four-year plans and portfolios. And we have other advisories that have started using commercial curriculum activities for character development. I can tell you that is *not* going over well with students, but I'm going to challenge you to ask them yourselves and consider what they're saying. I was going to repeat some rather cryptic quotes here, but I want you to ask them and hear it yourselves."

"Oh, c'mon. Lay it on us. At least give us a couple."

Mrs. Halverson looks around and sees a number of nods. She swallows hard. "Here goes then." She puts a transparency on the overhead. "You can read them for yourself."

Student 1: Forget the feel-good programs that are supposed to help self-esteem. We need honest respect, not phony "techniques."

Student 2: These canned lessons are all talk and no action. It's like the teacher needs a script to hide behind so he or she doesn't have to get real with us.

Student 3: You can't teach character and self-esteem. You have to model it. We can see through these teachers.

Student 4: That lesson about bullying. It was just useless. Did we start having these just to make sure the school wasn't going to get sued or something?

Student 5: Just be real and talk with us about real things. Why did we have that structured discussion about whether wearing hats in schools would be good or bad? We don't even wear hats here.

Silence. Throat clearing. A nervous cough. The comic relief comes from the back of the room in an Al Pacino voice. "OK. I confess. Take me away. But I'll never reveal my source."

After the laughter comes the real question. "All right, so at least we don't have two groups fighting over who gets to be in charge of advisories. That's a good thing. Now, you must have some ideas about what we should do."

"Yes, we do. We've talked about it a lot. We can do it within the master schedule you're used to, but it will be a different way of working with kids. We want to change advisories from one grade level to four grade levels, mixed, and keep the same kids together for all four years."

"You want one advisory group to have seniors, juniors, sophomores, and ninth graders all in the same room? Why?"

"Well, for one thing, it makes things easier for everyone because you only have to get four or five ninth graders started on their four-year plans. And it creates a built-in opportunity for senior mentors and ninth graders to get together. In fact, that's even less on you for helping everybody and more chances for students to help each other. And since a huge part of advisories is to really build relationships, you could really get to know students well in four years, couldn't you?"

"Good points. All true."

"But—that would mean a whole different group next year. One of my biggest problems, and I know I had a lot to say about it, was having a whole advisory full of kids I didn't have in any of my classes and didn't know."

"You're right—for this one year coming up, you might start with a whole new group, although we are going to try to keep a little nucleus in every advisory of students you now have. But the point is, after this first year, you would already know three-fourths of your advisory group, and only your ninth graders would be new."

"So, except for those of us who just have seniors now, people would keep some of their same kids until next year. And in the future, we'd all be taking some of the new ninth graders so they'd be more spread around."

"Yes, that's what we're thinking."

"OK, a different question. You said it would fit the current schedule. How would we do that?"

"We'd create a combination of advisory time and lunchtimes in the middle of the day. So there'd be a rotation of advisory time and lunch. That way they would see their friends from other advisories when they eat."

"What about getting together with their friends from their own grade? If this is all set up according to mixed grades, won't they miss being together as all seniors, and so on?"

"We did think about that, and we asked some students in our groups. We think there can be two configurations—sort of like when schedules have A and B days. There can be days when the rotation from advisories to lunch is by grade level so they can socialize. Or even have short class meetings during advisory time by pulling them out by grade level. So— like when the vendor comes about graduation announcements and robes and stuff—we can pull the seniors, and the rest of the advisory has time to work, have discussions, and so forth."

"That's a lot better than pulling them out of their classes. Sometimes the seniors get called out for a lot of stuff, but my classes also have juniors and some sophomores. Then I feel like I can't go ahead with my content while the seniors are gone."

"Yeah, that would be another benefit of this. I think it's worth trying."

"OK. We're going to continue working on it. I'd encourage you to run the idea by a few students that you're comfortable with and see what they think about our current advisories. Thanks for being open to this different idea."

"And, by the way, I'm one of the people with all ninth graders in advisory, and I want to thank the counselors and administrators for coming to our aid." As a round of applause breaks out, Mr. Spark heaves a sigh of relief. He remembers wondering if he'd have to become a referee between two groups. Instead, teacher leaders have moved from collegiality to true collaboration and created a win-win recommendation. But there's an issue among students demanding his attention.

The auditorium is full. Mr. Spark has gathered students, and they know he's concerned about something. The usual tomfoolery as they wait to start is hushed.

"Ladies and gentlemen. I want to start by reminding you that I've been proud of a lot of our accomplishments this year. As I told you in announcements a few weeks ago, our first semester results are awesome. We had our best attendance in the past four years! Discipline referrals are down—especially among ninth graders! D/F lists were the shortest I've ever seen! GPAs for every grade level are the highest of the last four years—and especially for our ninth graders! You are doing very well in many ways. But something sad has happened that makes me feel I have to tell you we still aren't where we need to be with relationships and caring for each other. So I've asked some students if they would let me share some things with you—just to remind you that we don't always know and appreciate the qualities of the people around us.

"I want Tom English to stand, please. You know Tom as one of our basketball stars. But did you know that Tom struggled academically and was barely making it in another school? That he came here for a fresh start as a sophomore and turned things around for himself? And that he's now pulling a 3.8 GPA? You didn't know, did you? There's Tom the athlete. There's also Tom the scholar. To really know Tom, you have to know the whole Tom.

"Now, will Ron Sharp please stand? The Ron you know is the scholar with the 4.0 GPA. Do you know that Ron lost a leg to cancer and navigates this place and all its stairs with an artificial leg? You didn't, did you? So maybe you admire his grades, but you don't know how much more there is to admire.

"Would Donna Barton please stand? How many of you know Donna? Not very many hands up. That's because Donna is very shy, and I could barely get her to agree to stand up. She made me promise four times that she wouldn't have to say anything. Donna has a 3.8 GPA and conducts some awesome community service projects. She helps arrange for volunteers to play with disabled youngsters on weekends when they don't have their center to go to. You should get to know the hidden Donna.

"Now, would Brady Stanton, please stand? Yes, you *have* noticed Brady. How could anyone miss a guy with huge spikes of hair poking out in all directions and such interesting attire? Did you know that Brady has taken five advanced placement exams and scored the top score of 5 on all of them? That's a Brady you didn't know, isn't it?

"And, last person in the spotlight. Would Clancy Smith please stand?"

There is no movement in the crowd, and Mr. Spark asks again. "Clancy, please stand." Heads are turned and looks are puzzled.

"Ladies and gentlemen, Clancy isn't standing. That's because he turned 16 yesterday and celebrated by quitting school. Some of you do know who Clancy is, because you've spoken to him—not spoken *with* him, but said things *to* him. The rest of you would have noticed a young man who was about 5'10" and weighed about 320 pounds. He was struggling academically and feeling awkward at school because of his weight. And you know some of the things he heard. Every student in this school is valuable, every one of you is valuable, and all of us are diminished when we lose even one. This is a short assembly. I don't have anything more to say to you. And I know what good hearts you have down inside, so I don't *need* to say a lot more to you. Our work at building a mutually respectful environment isn't done. I'm asking you to look around, see who there is that you will determine to get to know better, to really know. Reach out. Thanks. That's all."

Students leave in near silence. Teachers are thoughtful. Some know the assembly was short and ended quickly because Mr. Spark tries to hide the emotion he has for students that sometimes moves him close to tears.

QUESTIONS FOR REFLECTION

1. Changes are now being made in advisories that will benefit staff and students and move the school closer to its mission. What parameters did Mr. Spark set for their discussion? Do you think they would be at this stage if he had created mandates earlier?

2. Staff members decided to tap internal expertise rather than use consultants to learn about incorporating challenging material, critical thinking, and frequent assessment. What experiences over the last two years created readiness? What is the readiness level in your school, and how could you increase it? Which staff members would be identified by staff and students as most able to help others?

3. One role of principal as keeper of the culture is to reinforce school norms. Mr. Spark used a grade-level assembly to stress the importance of knowing each other and building relationships. How are the core values of your school reinforced by administrators, staff, and students?

4. As you answer these questions in your own thinking, what will you do to check the accuracy of your perceptions with students?

CONTENT FOR CONSIDERATION

Two of the cornerstone strategies in *Breaking Ranks II* (NASSP, 2004) relate to teachers working together and participating in ongoing professional development:

1. Implement schedules flexible enough to accommodate teaching strategies consistent with the ways students learn most effectively and that allow for effective teacher teaming and lesson planning.

2. Align the schoolwide comprehensive, ongoing professional development program and the individual Personal Learning Plans of staff members with the content knowledge and instructional strategies required to prepare students for graduation. (p. 6)

These activities are sometimes seen as disconnected from the overall school culture and school improvement work. Professional development occurs as "large-group instruction" planned at the school and/or district level or as individual, isolated effort through "continuous personal growth" plans done in isolation and often paid lip service only. The middle ground of "small-group" learning is virtually missing.

As Mike Schmoker (2004) asks, "How often over the PA or at an assembly or faculty meeting do we honor and celebrate such things as

- Teachers or teams who have increased student success in algebra or world history
- Students who met quarterly achievement or improvement goals
- Successful tutoring or remediation efforts that have helped struggling students to catch up with their classmates

- A decrease in the gap between socioeconomic groups in core or college-prep graduation rates
- Finding more effective, time-efficient ways to grade written work
- An engaging, effective lesson that produced high levels of success on a complex, intellectually engaging standard" (p. 6)

This is also the stuff of school culture, and "to truly institutionalize such a culture, perhaps our goal should be to turn an increasing proportion of professional development over to our effective teachers and teams, creating the kind of 'internal university' (Collins, 2001) so common in the corporate world" (p. 6).

Such an "internal university" might be designed like the Professional Teaching and Learning Cycle (PTLC) developed at the Southwest Educational Development Laboratory (SEDL). The PTLC is a process of collaboration and job-embedded professional development designed to improve teacher efficacy and instructional coherence. Small groups of teachers study standards and agree on expectations, select instructional strategies and resources that meet the standards and expectations, plan lessons that include a common assessment, implement the plan and analyze student work, and intervene to ensure that all students are proficient in the standards.

Protocols

Because this is a new way of interacting in most schools, Easton (cited in Blythe et al., 1999) recommends the use of tuning protocols to provide a structure for discussion of teacher and student work. The term itself provides reassurance about its purpose: fine-"tuning" to make good even better and "protocol" simply being a process to follow. Most protocols are designed to involve six to eight people with a presenter and facilitator for about an hour. The presenter has one or two key questions that he or she wants the others to help address. Participants provide both warm (positive) and cool (constructive) feedback. Another protocol, the Collaborative Assessment Conference, assists teachers in looking at the student work that results from their instruction (Blythe et al., 1999).

Protocols work well because the process protects the presenter from being intimidated or from being accused of bragging. "I'm just doing what the protocol asks me to." Following a described protocol greatly reduces rebuttals and polarization, ensures that all have time to talk, and allows the group to discuss at a deeper level and be more creative than occurs in more casual conversations.

Teacher Study Groups

The story of how Wyandotte High School developed a culture of professional growth is chronicled in *Breaking Ranks II* (NASSP, 2004, pp. 79–80). The seed was an informal teacher support group that began to meet after school for open discussion about teaching reading strategies. Teachers met weekly and exchanged materials, discussed implementation, shared successes and difficulties with their current classes, and discussed the effectiveness of the strategies they tried. As it evolved in trust and respect, teachers began to share their failures as well as their successes. They began to demonstrate lessons and offer suggestions for improvement, all with the hope of increasing student success. This focused work on reading then branched out to other teachers, and the entire staff is now involved in similar work in all content areas.

Peer Coaching

To support the implementation of the reading intervention and other instructional changes, the school then developed a peer coaching model. Substitute teachers are brought in two days per week so teachers can be released to observe in other classrooms. Teachers spend time collaboratively planning lessons, observing lessons, and participating in reflective conversations after lessons. The peer coaching system continues to evolve to include mentoring new teachers, collaborating with teachers in other schools, and embedding support from outside consultants into the classroom.

Peer coaching in the Bellingham (Washington) School District began in elementary schools, then moved into middle and high schools. Still in the beginning stages at the high schools, it has taken root at Fairhaven and Shuksan Middle Schools, where a focus has been on monitoring student learning closely enough to use flexible grouping and individual conferences to address specific student needs. In order to work with individuals and small groups, procedures for planning and working independently have been taught to students. Chuck Davange, math teacher, commented on a videotape for a school board visit, "What I'm getting out of the training is basically an ability to assess my kids, and know where they're at as individuals, and know where they're at as groups, and really be able to react to it. That's what's been most powerful for me. Having my classroom set up in such a way that I can react to my kids' performance. I can structure my assignments so that I measure my kids' performance and really know where they're at and then choose my teaching so that I'm meeting my kids' needs. I've seen—and my data shows—an increase in my kids' performance. My kids are happier and I'm happier and I feel like there's real learning going on at multiple levels in my room, instead of just teaching at one level and it's up to the kids to come up to there. That's been the most valuable for me" (personal communication, n.d.).

Mary Jo Stuckrath, eighth-grade core teacher, adds, "Probably the biggest 'aha' for me this year has been with my monitoring notes and being able to use those and determine what skills the kids really do have and what skills they need. And that has led me to really have effective small group instruction time, which has proven to be a more effective use of my time. The other big change in my classroom because of what I've learned is that I run a literacy block now instead of a subject-by-subject time frame. That has facilitated small-group instruction. It also has led to the kids' planning for their own time within that literacy block. And they're planning for their time over a week and noting when their assignments are due, versus the period by period approach and this assignment is due at the end of the period" (personal communication, n.d.).

A STUDENT GETS THE LAST WORD

Their students see the difference in their classrooms and in their own learning. Says one, "I think this new system seems really nice because our classroom seems to be more laid back instead of like a strict schedule. I can get things done in the priority order for me instead of the whole class's priority. So if I'm done with some things, I can work on what I need to and this is more prioritizing on my own" (personal communication, n.d.).

Another adds, "I think that this is different—from like last time when you were teaching us all as one—now you're teaching us as individuals— it's better. It teaches us to be independent and kinda like be our own teachers. We can get more work done. Instead of working on just one thing and sometimes not even finishing it, now we have all the time to spend on just one thing if we want to. It's kind of teaching us to be more responsible for our work" (personal communication, n.d.).

April, Year 2

The Stakes Are High

"**M**r. Spark, Mr. Spark. What did they decide about advisories?"

"Hi, Morris. This topic of advisories seems to have been your theme for several months now. It matters an awful lot to you, doesn't it?"

"Well, YEA-AH! If it doesn't turn out right, how does the mentoring program work through the year? Where do ninth graders start their four-year plans? Where do seniors work on their major portfolio project and do their resumes and stuff?"

"Morris, I'm glad to tell you that you can rest your mind on all of those. The teachers had a lot of informal discussions after the faculty meeting. Some of them talked with students and heard various versions of the same things you just said. So we're moving forward with the sort of scheduling that Mrs. Halverson and Mr. O'Brien recommended. There will be four-year advisories, and they will incorporate all those things you've talked about."

"And will they dump that canned stuff some of them were using?"

"Oh, I think so. There are a few who don't have a strong comfort level with how to handle this part of their day, but others have volunteered to team up with them and help them plan. And like you said, students can identify tasks they want to work on together and issues they want to discuss."

"That's good. Because that brings the relationships and citizenship into it too. Like in my advisory, we talked about the boundaries for open campus lunch. Some kids didn't understand why we can go toward downtown or east toward the fast-food places but not across the streets toward the north or west. We talked about the elementary school over there, and the senior residences, and they realized that's part of how we respect others. And we have enough options for places to eat. They were going to take a proposal for change to the House of Representatives but then decided not to. That's the kind of stuff that makes school relevant and lets us develop real character."

"I agree, Morris. That's an excellent example. You have really contributed great ideas and a lot of time and energy to our school. When you graduate next month, you'll be leaving it a better place."

"Well, remember, I have a brother coming here next year. He's a little more shy than me, and I want to make sure it really *will* be Knownwell High School. These new advisories will help assure that every student *is* 'known well.'"

"Hey, Mr. Spark. I've got a good one for you. You know what the tenth graders are saying? They're saying this place has a sixth R that they never voted for. You've really done a job on them."

"A sixth R? You mean another one besides the three R's and relationships and responsibility? What would that be?"

"They're saying 'relentless.' About the state test. I mean, they know you've been talking about it all year. But now you went to every 10th-grade class and asked them what they had heard about the test and whether they thought it mattered to them as individuals, to their parents, to the school. You connected it to the Collective Commitments—respect others, respect this place, respect your chances. And the way you listen to students, well, it makes them ready to listen to you. So when you say 'I need you to come and take the test and take the test seriously,' they don't want to let you down."

"And they call that relentless?"

"No, that was just the preliminaries. The relentless part is how you and the assistant principals and the counselors called up the parents of every kid who was absent and told them it was important and made sure they knew when the makeup day is for the part they missed. Now, *that's* relentless."

"You've got me there, Morris. We do seem to have everyone's attention. I know we've had great participation, and as we're starting to get the tests ready to return, I haven't heard about any blank ones or goofing off on the multiple-choice bubbles or anything like that. I'm always so amazed at how students come through when we really *ask* you to."

"Well, Mr. Spark, you know it's because you and most of the teachers here, you respect us and listen to us. In some schools, kids just feel like a cog in a machine. So if the principal would ask them to do something, they'd wait until you walked away and then behind your back they'd say 'blank you.' You know the blank, right?"

"I'm afraid I do know the blank, Morris. And I'm sure glad I don't hear it here."

"So—when will you find out if we did a lot better this year with all the relentless stuff on the state test?"

"The results will come late in the summer. We won't have them by graduation, but you call me or check the Web site before you head off to college and I'm just sure they will have gone up."

"Good job, Mr. Spark."

"Well, that's a mutual 'good job' to you and the student leadership, Morris."

"So this is my plan." Teri is concluding her presentation to her advisory group. "I have a part-time job waitressing for the summer, and then I'm going to keep working at it when I start the community college. For a while, I wanted to be a sign language interpreter. I've heard that it's a good way to help young autistic children learn to communicate. But in Mrs. Donnelly's strategies class, I learned about my strengths and challenges, and I've decided that sign language interpretation is something that is very fast paced and could be stressful. I need to do something that has a more predictable pace to it.

"So my goal now is to get an associate's degree that will give me the qualifications to be an office assistant and make sure that things are filed right and people are listened to, and communications give a good impression. I've been helping in the office here, and people think I'm doing a good job. I would work in a doctor's office where I could help people who already have enough stress to deal with and need to be treated with the kind of respect I've had here. When I talked with Joe and some other graduates at Home for the Holidays, I realized that I can take extra time to get the two-year degree if I need to. And then when I have a job as an office assistant, I can discover if I want to take more college and work toward being an office manager.

"I can't say how glad I am that I get to graduate from this high school. In a lot of schools, people automatically think that if you have an IEP, you won't go to college. They steer you away from hard courses because they want to protect you from tough challenges. But in this school, I took some hard courses that interested me, and I went to the extra help periods, and I learned that I could be my own advocate and talk with teachers about what I need to help me learn. I'm not helpless, and I don't have to just do boring, easy stuff. So I want to thank my school, my principal, my teachers, and all of you fellow students who have respected me and encouraged me."

QUESTIONS FOR REFLECTION

1. What strategies were used to develop a culture around the state assessment? How is "testing time" handled in your school? Are the incentives extrinsic or intrinsic?

2. Mr. Spark and Morris indicated that when you listen to students, they'll come through for you. Do you believe that's true? Why? Why not? How does it look in your school?

3. How has Teri changed over the last two years? What factors contributed to the changes? How does her school experience affect the way she views the future?

4. As you answer these questions in your own thinking, what will you do to check the accuracy of your perceptions with students?

CONTENT FOR CONSIDERATION

Listening and Leadership

Morris reassures Mr. Spark that students will respond to his requests, because he has listened to and respected them. Dennis Sparks (2006), former executive director of the National Staff Development Council, writes, "Few things would improve the quality of school leadership more . . . than leaders spending more of their time truly listening in a purely receptive way to those with whom they work. Few leadership actions hold a similar level of promise to promote change in leaders themselves, to influence others, and to dramatically improve relationships in schools. And few things are more challenging for leaders than the discipline of careful, attentive listening because of the fast pace and fragmentation of their workdays" (p. 2). His article includes a quote from Parker Palmer: "What the human heart really wants is not to be fixed, but to be heard and received."

True listening is such an essential and rare skill that Stephen Covey (2004) has made it "the eighth habit" of people who are moving from effectiveness to greatness. It takes intentional purpose and practice to develop the skills and apply them on a consistent basis. The National Staff Development Council provides tools such as "Listen Fully" in its publications for school leaders, *Tools* and *Results*.

Students on Test Prep

Listening is most difficult when the information is unexpected, unsupportive, or comes from an unfamiliar source. Such was the case in the Philadelphia School District when student members of Youth United for Change requested meetings with district leaders on the topic of test preparation (Gewertz, 2006). Their request was prompted by complaints from peers that they had to leave core subjects to attend preparation sessions for state and district tests. Through their research, these students learned that the district had selected classmates who were near the top of various performance categories in hopes that additional help would move their scores into the next category and help the school avoid sanctions. Results of their survey of 200 fellow students revealed that 8 of 10 students disagreed with being taken out of major subject classes for test preparation. One senior stated, "You would think I would be happy to get the help, but I enjoyed social studies. And it made me feel bad for the other students who needed help and weren't chosen" (p. 12).

The district agreed to revise its policy on test preparation and test administration. Test preparation will be part of regular class work, and elective sessions and afterschool sessions on test-taking tips may also be offered. The district pledged to make test preparation available to all students who want it. In addition, students suggested that math classrooms be used for the English tests and English classrooms for math tests so teachers wouldn't have to remove materials that might be considered helpful. They recommended posters to clarify the guidelines of what is and isn't acceptable during test taking and suggested the addition of a second proctor in each test setting.

This is not the first time Youth United for Change has been successful in projecting the student voice. Working with individual schools, they have won stronger course offerings, better lighting for a dangerous route to and from one high school, and more money for technology at another.

On the opposite coast, students at West Valley High School in Washington State participate in weekly focus groups that discuss current issues being addressed in the Coordinating Council. These range from the structure of the mentor (advisory) program to a possible change from one to two lunch periods, to ways of increasing the sense of community within the school. Future extensions of the focus groups are being considered, such as including administrators so they can hear student ideas firsthand. Another idea is to use the focus groups for discussion about how to redesign the overall decision-making structures of the school.

A STUDENT GETS THE LAST WORD

Freshman Rocky Rutter has been participating in West Valley's process. He got involved because he wanted to help shape what happened at his school:

Instead of letting school happen to me, I thought it would be better to get involved and make a difference. I can take what I've been hearing from other students and provide a voice for those who can't participate. . . . Schools exist for student learning. Who better to know how students learn best than students? To not listen to students is illogical. Besides, students have a lot to say. (Lambert, 2003, pp. 2–3)

21

May, Year 2

Morris Graduates

"Hey, Morris. When's the next time you and all the Table Ten crew are getting together? I've got something I want to show you."

"That's cool. And good timing. It just so happens that we're getting together at dismissal time tomorrow to make sure we have phone numbers and e-mail addresses and ways to keep in touch when we graduate and get cut off the school Internet."

"Perfect. I'll catch up with you then."

Mr. Spark hurries back to his office to finish a chart he's making that will show the results of work that began back when Morris asked about accreditation.

"Mr. Spark, we're over here. What did you want to show us?"

"Here it is." Mr. Spark gives them each a copy of his results chart. "I've been trying to create a one-page picture of the things we've worked on in the last couple of years and how it's made a difference. Since you've been so involved, I wanted to share it with you and make sure you got your own copy."

"That's awesome. Wow. I remember looking at all that data. And now here's data that show we accomplished something. And . . . Mr. Spark—you

Figure 21.1 Report of School Improvement Progress: Knownwell High School, End of Year 2 (Preliminary)

Priority Area: Three R's (to provide diverse and challenging experiences, assure that all students master essential skills, and practice critical thinking)

Strategies	Evidence of Implementation	Evidence of Impact
* Five Elements of Powerful Teaching * Thinking strategies for reading comprehension * Departmental help periods before/after school * Teacher study groups for unit and lesson planning	* Administrator walk-throughs show increasing use of Five Elements, ranging from 20% to 78% * Help periods attended by average of 15 students per period * All teachers trained in thinking strategies for reading; plans developed for protocols to work together on unit and lesson plans	* Student survey shows use of Five Elements and some integration of thinking strategies * D/F lists reduced by 35% * State test results (to be added in August)

Priority Area: Relationships (in a mutually respectful environment)

Strategies	Evidence of Implementation	Evidence of Impact
* Realignment of counselors by alphabet * Ninth-grade mentors * Advisories	* Letters to families that explained realignment and identified counselor * Mentor program established; met three times in August, once in September * Advisories incorporated into master schedule; being modified to four-year configuration	* Discipline referrals for ninth graders down by 60% * Attendance rate increased from 91% to 95%

Priority Area: Responsibility (all students master essential skills, produce high quality work, and practice responsible citizenship)

Strategies	Evidence of Implementation	Evidence of Impact
* Expanded student government—House of Representatives * Collective Commitments and common classroom rules * Advisories * Four-year plans and portfolios	* House of Representatives established; 35 groups represented * Collective Commitments affirmed and published * Common rules identified and shared by mentors and teachers * Advisories incorporated into master schedule; being modified to four-year configuration * Current ninth graders developed plans and started portfolios	* Discipline referrals for ninth graders down by 60% * Attendance rate increased from 91% to 95%

wrote a 'Thank you' on the bottom here and signed it. All we did was talk to you. You're the one who should be thanked. You listened."

"Morris, I've always tried to listen and care about students. But you helped the whole staff begin to see how students could really contribute to the real work of our mission. And it's grown and evolved and spread throughout the school. This is a legacy you've given to our school."

"I see that state test results have to be added when you get them in August. I'm going to be checking in with you, Mr. Spark. I think we'll have something to celebrate there."

"I think so too, Morris. And as I said when I was being so 'relentless,' as you put it, that is an important indicator. But for me, the real indicator is watching you all march across that stage and get your diplomas. We've had some students move away, but every senior who started in August and is still in our community is going to make the march on Friday night. And you're going to do great things with your lives—that's the biggest indicator for me."

"Well, don't get all teary-eyed yet. We're still around a few more days. And we'll be coming back a lot to keep you on your toes."

Mr. Spark is gathering his notes for the graduation ceremony about to begin. He glances around his office and smiles. His reputation for being emotional about students is known well, and this year's class of seniors conspired to gain entry and filled every horizontal surface with boxes of Kleenex. He notices a package that looks like a framed plaque or picture. Glancing at his watch, he realizes it's time to check that staff members are lined up in the Choir Room and students are assembled and properly out-fitted in the hallways. First, he pats his pockets to make sure there are several crisply folded handkerchiefs within easy access—just in case.

The gymnasium is crammed to the rafters. The graduates have completed their procession, and the customary speeches have taken place. Mr. Spark announces that seniors also have the tradition of choosing a speaker who may not have any of the official roles and status but who they want to hear from. He doesn't finish his introduction as the group begins to chant "Mor-RIS! Mor-RIS! Mor-RIS!"

His speech is in character—short and self-deprecating. He concludes, "I'm only up here because I had some ideas, and Mr. Spark and you and our teachers took it way farther than anything I thought about. So I just want to thank you all and make sure you remember three things. Help me out." His classmates respond loudly, "Respect OTHERS. Respect THIS PLACE. Respect our CHANCES."

Graduates' names are called to receive their diplomas. It's a time-consuming process, as each and every senior stops to hug Mr. Spark. All applaud as the classmate who lost his leg lifts his robe to sport his new prosthesis. All laugh as the football fullback lifts the principal off the ground and twirls him around. And all eyes are moist as the class rises in a standing ovation when he declares them officially graduated from Knownwell High School. They exit through the tunnel created by two rows of teachers—more handshakes, high fives, and hugs as they leave this gym for the last time.

Mr. Spark returns to his office and picks up the gift-wrapped package that's been waiting for his attention. It is indeed a framed document—but not a famous quote or engraved plaque. It is a letter from a student, hand-written in careful calligraphy.

> *Dearest Mr. Spark:*
>
> *What a journey it has been. I must say that not a single second of my high school experience would have been as enjoyable if it weren't for you. You are an amazing person full of hope and inspiration and I completely adore you. Students look to you for guidance when they are lost, and you never fail to point them in the right direction. You are the heart of this school. Students find themselves avoiding trouble, not afraid of being punished, but in fear of disappointing you, because you have discovered the secret to creating a fabulous school. That secret is developing relationships with every student and making sure you know all of their names. You impress me a great deal with that kindness and love you share with every one of your students and faculty. Because of this, you deserve much more than I could ever give, but what I can say is thanks and I love you for being the wonderful man that you are. You will always be remembered and greatly missed as we embark on the journey of the rest of our lives. Thank you and good-bye from the class of 2004.*
>
> *— Briana*

The frame has glass on both sides, because the back is covered with short comments and signatures from other seniors.

We couldn't have asked for a better leader. Thank you for all you do.
— Jim

You rock—Maddy

You are awesome! Thank you for making high school its best.—Chris

Thanks for the great inspirational speeches.
—Matina

Mr. Spark, you're awesome.—Mark

To the best principal ever . . . well . . . yeah, ever!
—Aaron

You're rad, dude!—Luke

You're the best ever! I'll miss you, but don't worry, I'll stop by to say hi!—
Alyssa

What an amazing principal—you are making everyone enjoy their high school experience.
Thank you. —Melanie

Good job.—Janie

You put the "pal" in "principal."
Thank you.—Megan

We cannot thank you enough!
—Julie, Kate, & Azubo

You are truly a man of God.
—Jackie

Thanks for the memories and your leadership.
—David

You're the best! High school was cool.—Caitlin

Thank you for four excellent years!
—Evan

Thanks for everything.—Sarah

I like you.—David

Thank you. —Shannon

You're the man; thanks for being the best principal ever.—Shannon

I love you so much.
See you on Saturday!
—Brandon

Thanks so much for everything. You are THE MAN!!—Rylan

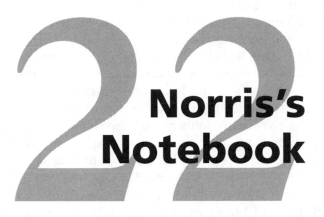

22 Norris's Notebook

The spiral-bound notebook is now rumpled, dog-eared, and overflowing with data graphs, clippings from newsletters, scraps of announcements, and Post-it notes of memories shared by students, teachers, and graduates. Norris remembers how thin and clean it was on his first day at Knownwell High School—when he set himself the task of finding out what Morris did to become a hero of the school culture. In the mentoring program, they had told him it was a good idea to keep a journal. His became the journal of a school's journey. And in the process, Norris found another hero. On the inside back cover, the last available space in the notebook, Norris pastes the press release announcing Mr. Spark's selection as a finalist for national Principal of the Year. The clipping refers to his previous honor as state Principal of the Year and also mentions the county Peace Builder award he recently received.

A line from a song runs through Norris's head. "It takes two, ba-by-ee. It takes two." It reminds him of the need for both sender and receiver, author and audience. The student voice began with Morris taking the risk to ask questions about his school. But it wouldn't have gone anywhere without a receptive adult who listened.

"If a tree falls in the forest and no one is there, does it make a sound? If student voice is strong and clear and no one listens, can it make a difference?" Norris knows the answer. He has friends in other schools where the students' voices are heard only by each other.

At Knownwell High School, it started with a student and a principal. The student created a nucleus that grew to be the Table Ten group. The principal began to talk with a few teachers. The students began to talk with a few teachers directly. Those teachers talked to other teachers. Other students began to talk with the Table Ten group and with each other. They didn't break up the school into smaller units. They just broke down the walls of silence and isolation.

As Norris leafs back through his collection of memories and quotes, he wonders what purpose it could serve. He's answered his own question about what Morris did to become such a big deal—but it seems like somebody else should know. Maybe other students and principals could learn how to involve students as stakeholders and create this kind of school for more kids. And Norris wonders how he can find his own voice—his own way to contribute to the high school he loves.

"One of the things Morris did was work on graphs and stuff. Yuck. I'm not a numbers guy. And he gave presentations to teachers and speeches with Joe and Mr. Spark. Please, no, I just can't go there. All I'm any good at is just . . . all I can do is . . . write.

"Maybe I can pull this together and write it down. So other people will know what happened here. Maybe it can be my major project for my portfolio. And maybe that will help to make sure that people don't forget what we've done here. It will be a story that can be told to ninth graders so they know how special this place is and how it got to be that way and what they need to do to keep it special.

"I'll need a way of organizing it so people can see the big picture of the different things that students were involved in and how all the parts fit together. Maybe that can be a graphic organizer. If it's one of the powerful learning strategies, it should work well as a communication tool too.

"First the mission statement got written and Mr. Spark brought it back and forth to the students for their reaction. So I'll put the six key phrases that they agreed on right at the top. Later on the students talked about beliefs and what kind of school they wanted, so I'll put the three 'respect' statements there, too. That's my first drawing." (See Figure 22.1.)

"The School Portfolio had all that data that Morris crunched. Since that was the other starting point, I'll put it on the bottom at the left. And I'll make notes of some of the stuff they discussed—test scores and attendance and discipline, plus people's thoughts on the Teen Survey and the staff perceptions. That gives me another component on my diagram." (See Figure 22.2.)

"Teachers talked about the data, and of course they thought the problems were all on the students at first. And the students' complaints were sort of aimed at the teachers. I'll put a space for Concerns on the diagram. That sounds a lot better than problems or complaints. It sure was cool that they realized it all matched up. When it came right down to it, the adults and the kids really wanted the same things." (See Figure 22.3.)

"Once they focused in on specific concerns, they came up with some shared goals to work on. They started talking about the five R's, but I'll call them Priorities so my diagram could fit any school. Hard to believe it took half a year to get that far. It's a good thing Mr. Spark was patient." (See Figure 22.4.)

Figure 22.1 Knownwell High School Mission and Collective Commitments

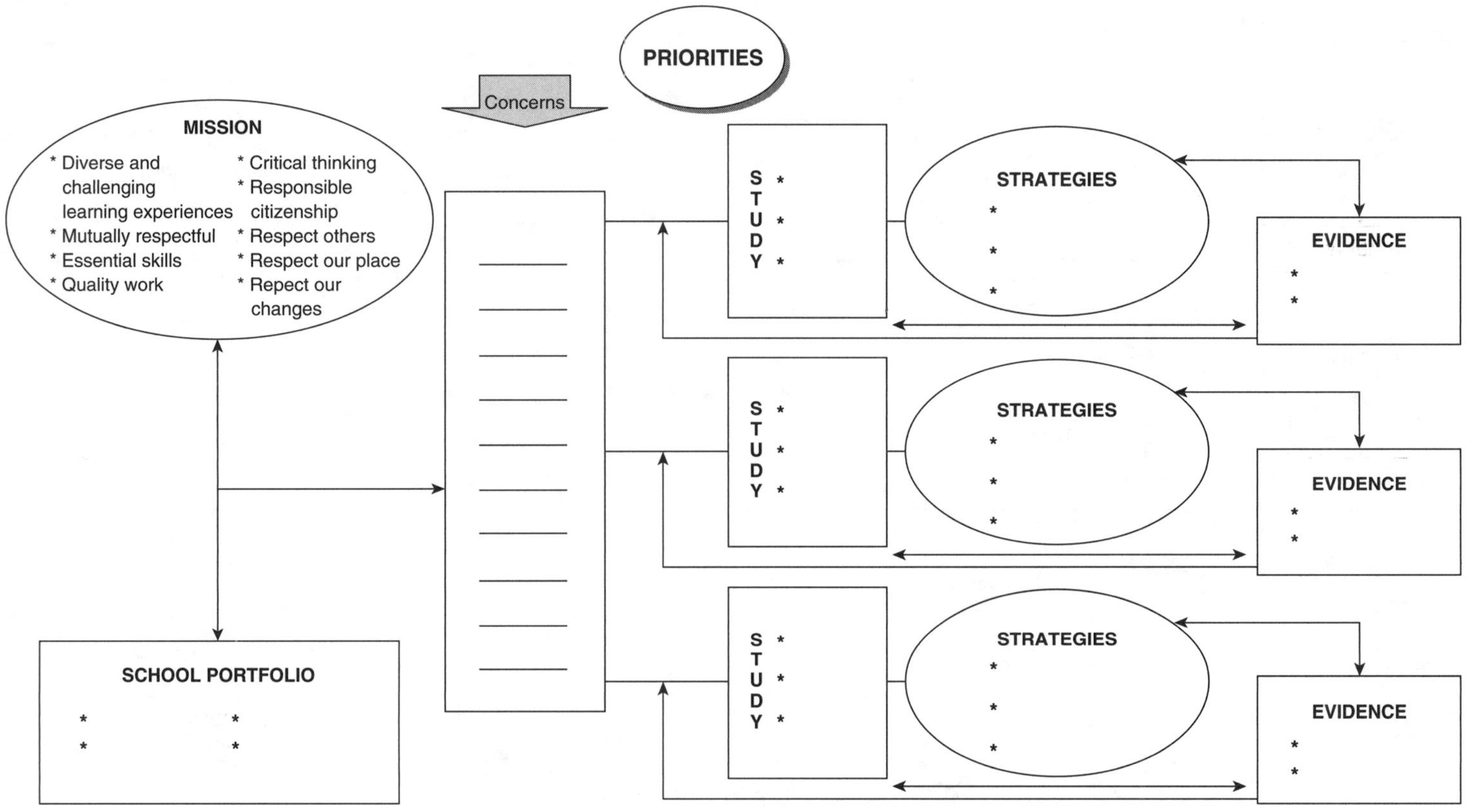

Figure 22.2 Knownwell High School Portfolio Highlights

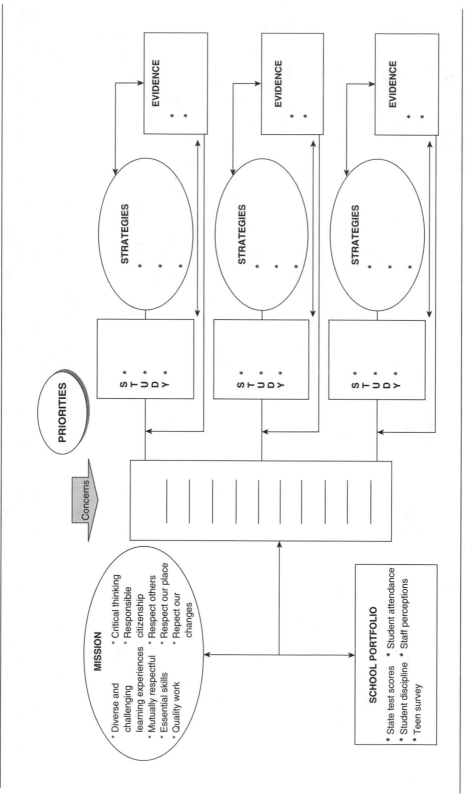

Figure 22.3   Knownwell High School Staff and Student Concerns

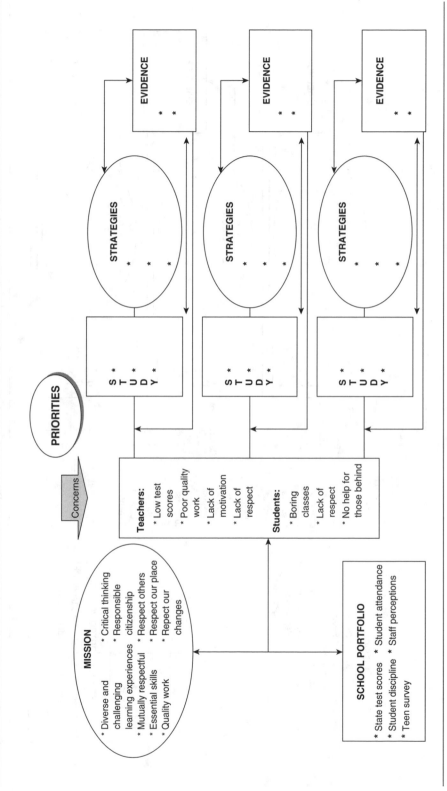

Figure 22.4 Knownwell High School Priorities

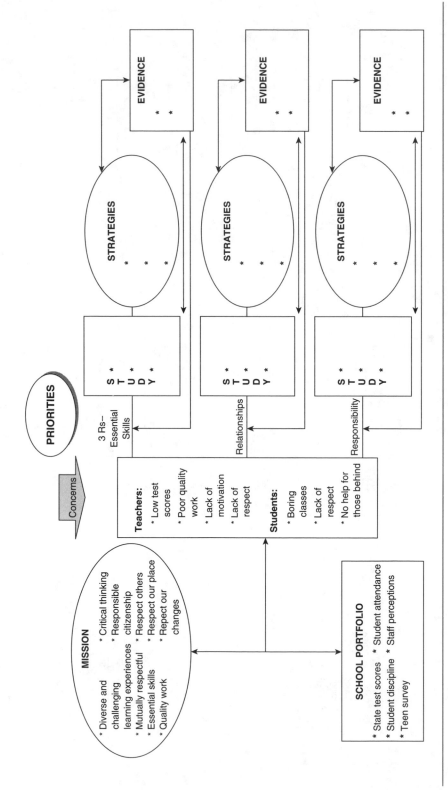

"Then the teachers had an inservice day to study what to do. The kids got invited to come to the study groups. They zeroed right in on the problems of the ninth graders, and they read some of the same books. And they got more input from students. By then, students could open up and be pretty specific about what they thought would make classes and the school better. I should be sure there's a space on here to remind people not to rush into plans without really digging into their data and studying research." (See Figure 22.5.)

"Once they had learned more about what to do, they started picking strategies to help with each of the five R's. The essential skills were the first 3 Rs. I wish I'd been there for the teacher fight—oops, I mean dialogue—about best teaching practices. But it's amazing. The 5 Elements posters are still up in the classrooms and now they're getting to the hardest one about assessment and feedback. And my teachers talk about accessing text and comprehension strategies and how they think about things as they read. Some of the collegebound kids are even trying to get into Power Reading.

"By the end of the first year, they were changing counselors and setting up a mentor program so students could help students—and they put more time in homerooms. I'll connect those strategies to the fourth R—Relationships.

"To give students more responsibility—or to get them to take more responsibility—they really used the Collective Commitments. There was no doubt about it. Students got on each other and when that overweight kid got bullied and quit, Mr. Spark let the kids know that wasn't living up to the expectations. They expanded student governance and came up with common rules. Kinda scary how that seems so logical but it was such a big deal. I'll put the four-year plans there, too—even though they didn't get added until the second year.

"That's one thing I got out of this. It's like the improvement plan is never done, it's always getting improved itself. Like in the second year, advisories really weren't going so good and they changed them second semester. Now it's the third year and they finally seem like real advisories." (See Figure 22.6.)

"That's pretty much all of the strategies we've tried. That part of the organizer seems to have kept evolving. I guess that's because Mr. Spark was always monitoring things, like doing the walk-throughs and showing teachers the numbers. And some of the strategies led to more data—not just the usual stuff like grades and test scores, but the groups needed to check counselor logs to be sure they were really doing what they said they would do, and they had to survey students after a couple of years to see if they felt more connections. They were hoping that better attendance and participation, and lower discipline referrals, would provide evidence that kids were taking more responsibility." (See Figure 22.7.)

"I can see why that chart Mr. Spark gave to Morris had columns for evidence of implementation and impact. It's implementation if you can see people doing what's in the plan, and it's impact if you can see it's making a difference. I can add on the state test scores now. Morris didn't have them yet when he graduated." (See Figure 22.8.)

Figure 22.5 Knownwell High School Study Areas

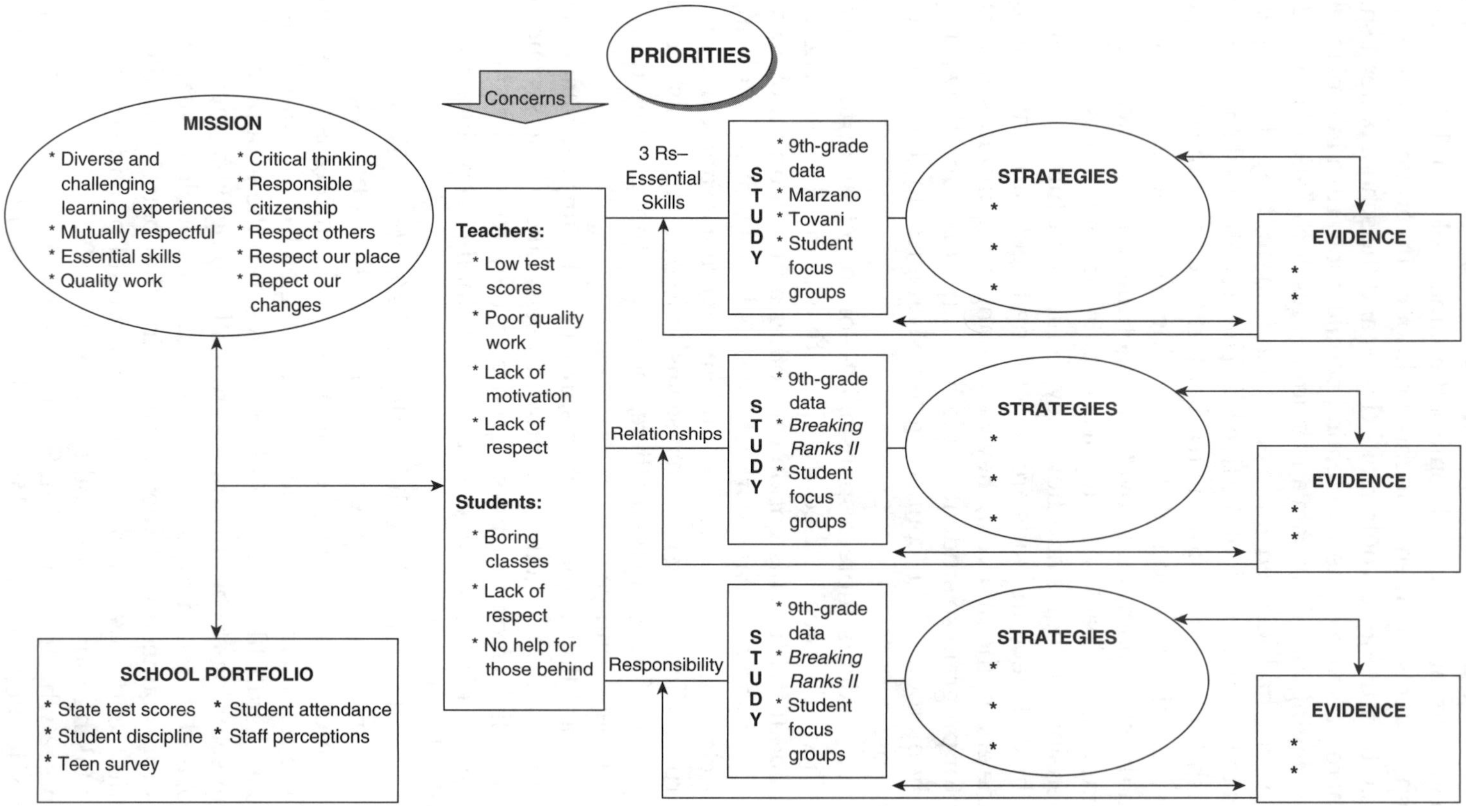

Figure 22.6 Knownwell High School Strategies

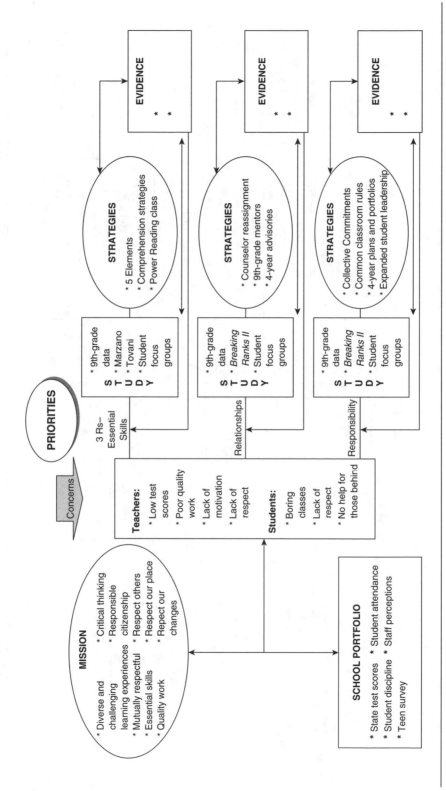

Figure 22.7 Knownwell High School's Complete Improvement Plan

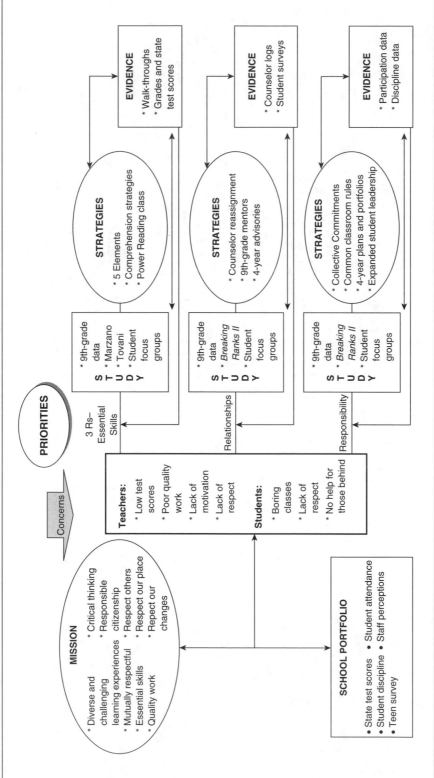

Figure 22.8 Report of School Improvement Progress: Knownwell High School, End of Year 2 (Final)

Priority Area: Three R's (to provide diverse and challenging experiences, assure that all students master essential skills, and practice critical thinking)

Strategies	Evidence of Implementation	Evidence of Impact

* Five Elements of Powerful Teaching
* Thinking strategies for reading comprehension
* Departmental help periods before/after school
* Teacher study groups for unit and lesson planning
	* Administrator walk-throughs show increasing use of Five Elements; ranging from 20% to 78 %
	* Help periods attended by average of 15 students per period
	* All teachers trained in thinking strategies for reading; plans developed for protocols to work together on unit and lesson plans
		* Student survey shows use of Five Elements and some integration of thinking strategies
		* D/F lists reduced by 35%
		* Proficient on State Tests State Average:
		  Reading 55% to 89% 72%
		  Math 42% to 72% 47%
		  Writing 55% to 83% 65%
		  Science 35% to 56% 36%

Priority Area: Relationships (in a mutually respectful environment)

Strategies	Evidence of Implementation	Evidence of Impact
* Realignment of counselors by alphabet * Ninth-grade mentors * Advisories	* Letters to families that explained realignment and identified counselor * Mentor program established; met three times in August, once in September * Advisories incorporated into master schedule; being modified to four-year configuration	* Discipline referrals for ninth graders down by 60% * Attendance rate increased from 91% to 95%

Priority Area: Responsibility (all students master essential skills, produce high quality work, and practice responsible citizenship)

Strategies	Evidence of Implementation	Evidence of Impact
* Expanded student government—House of Representatives * Collective Commitments and common classroom rules * Advisories * Four-year plans and portfolios	* House of Representatives established; 35 groups represented * Collective Commitments affirmed and published * Common rules identified and shared by mentors and teachers * Advisories incorporated into master schedule; being modified to four-year configuration * Current ninth graders developed plans and started portfolios	* Discipline referrals for ninth graders down by 60% * Attendance rate increased from 91% to 95%

"WOW! In two years, that's a lot of impact. Maybe that data will help make other schools want to know what happened here. It seems like just about every school is trying to figure out what to do to get better.

"Well, Morris did data and I don't. But he wasn't one to write things down. So I guess my voice can get expressed my way. I can make sure people don't forget. And I'll write that it doesn't matter what the name of your school is—any school can get to be a place where every student is *known well.*"

Epilogues. . .

From a Principal

My name is Steve Clarke, and I'm Mr. Spark—sort of. The physical settings such as the Flag Patio, the Commons, and the Choir Room are my world. Students like Morris, Joe, Mike, Gloria, Teri, and Tim walk through my doors and my life every day. Holcomb has woven elements from other schools into the composite, but the heart of what happened at Knownwell High School is similar to what happened at Bellingham High School. The main difference is that Knownwell started their transition work midstream, while our work at Bellingham High started during a two-year closure, renovation, and subsequent reopening of the school. I wanted to have student involvement in the planning right from the start, so I placed announcements in the daily bulletins at the four middle schools and two high schools from which students would be coming. I stated, "Any future student of BHS can apply to be part of the BHS Leadership Team." I was hoping for 25–30, but 121 applied. I asked them to write their experiences and the decisions they would want to be involved in. I ended up taking all 121 kids. They knew we would need to reconsider the old Native American mascot and wanted input on that. They also wanted input on student activities that would be offered. I remember the top six were dance, drama, pep club, literary magazine, power lifting, and video journalism. You have to admit that's quite a range of interests being expressed and addressed right off the bat.

When we gathered in the community college gym, I asked the students to talk about what makes a great high school. What are we willing to commit to? We knew we wanted to be different from the old BHS and sought out ways to make that happen. With the Collective Commitments as our base, we built (and continue to build) a program that meets the needs of all kids. Students clearly voiced their opinion that respecting all members of the BHS community would be vital to our success, and they were right!

We established our student government (like the House of Reps requiring 30 signatures) prior to our reopening. As many know, advisories have been around forever, with mixed results. We knew that and, as a result, have forms of advisories that are geared toward the need at the time. Our LINK program connects upperclassmen with frosh as they enter our program. All of our seniors are mentored by a staff member. Every staff member has four seniors to assist along the way with their culminating project.

We used student surveys, and their voice was heard loud and clear. Staff recognized the need for changes and faced them and responded. Our success can be traced back to the fact that we have a terrific staff and amazing students. With a staff that is focused on what is best for kids, anything can happen. With a positive school culture, kids want to be in school. When they want to be there and they know you believe the best in them, they rise to the expectations set before them. Our students are kids from our neighborhoods—some poor, some wealthy—but they know that everyone is as important as anyone else. When you have that core belief and acceptance at the heart level, a positive culture is the by-product. We have almost no fights (five in six years). I believe that's because we are one—not separated into the haves and have-nots that resent each other. Our kids believe and live out our Collective Commitments every day. Our staff members know that these commitments are the bedrock of our success and live by them as well.

Creating a student-focused culture and listening to student voice can be done anywhere. If we can do it, anyone can. We are just normal people trying to serve and educate kids to the best of our abilities—but it is about the kids, not the adults. As soon as we make it about anything other than the kids, we are all in trouble. But I believe with a healthy staff that is willing to take a serious look at who we are and what we are doing that isn't working, anything can happen.

The sad truth is that we are the ones getting in our way. We like to think that there is a "bad guy" out there who is really keeping us from doing the great work we all inwardly want to do—work that makes a difference in the lives of kids! But often this work requires taking a good hard look at who we are and what we have always done—and changing it. Since that is often painfully hard work, we instead shift our attention to outside influences and blame them—the district office, state and federal mandates (especially those that are unfunded), uninvolved parents, class sizes, the elementary schools, the middle schools, poverty, lack of adequate resources, and on and on. No doubt there is some truth in each of these, but we must not let these excuses immobilize us.

My challenge to principals would be this: cultivate a healthy culture before you do anything else. You cannot sustain effective change without a positive culture to support it. I believe we have underestimated this in schools, and it has not allowed most schools to move forward. Instead of healthy growth for kids' sake, we have kingdoms and infighting where a lack of trust rules the day. Be vulnerable. Let folks know that you do not have all the answers, that you have blown it many times. Apologize (even publicly, if necessary) if you have wronged someone or taken your team off track. Own your mistakes, and folks will begin to own theirs. Ask staff and students what they think is working and what is not—and be prepared to get beat up a bit by their honesty, but don't take it too personally.

Be the person you want your students and staff to be. Believe the best in them, and they will believe the best in you—eventually. If we could see our work as more of an inverted triangle, with us at the bottom supporting teachers, who are in turn supporting kids (who are at the top), we would make more of a difference every day in our work. Last, listen and be with the kids whenever and wherever possible. I try to be with them before school, in classes, at breaks, lunches, and at the door as they leave—thanking them for their contribution. I want to be at their games and concerts to celebrate their successes. The more we are where they are, the better handle we have on what we are really doing and what they are really thinking and feeling about their school.

To teachers, I would say this: you are the heart and soul of every school. A good school has good teachers, and a great school has great teachers. Our goal has been to have kids "click on all cylinders all day," which means they go through their entire day with a great teacher in every classroom, every period. For high school teachers specifically, I encourage you to open your practice to your peers. I think teaching high school can be an isolating existence. Be a part of a Critical Friends Group or Lesson Study, where you work regularly with your colleagues on talking about your practice and the work you do every day with your kids. Encourage your peers to come in and watch you teach and talk about what they saw. I know this is risky, but our staff has found great support in our instructional coaching and peer groups. Be healthy. Take care of yourselves and your families. If you are not healthy, you will not last—and we need great teachers that are in it for the long haul.

And to students, I would say this: don't think that you cannot make a difference in your schools. Margaret Mead once said, "Never doubt that a small group of committed citizens can change the world. Indeed that is the only thing that ever has." You have the power to change your school—for good or for bad. Without a doubt, our students have helped shape who we are as a school. Their ideas, input, and talents have been foundational in our success. The key is to find an access point for your voice to be heard. If it is your principal, great! Meet with him or her and put your ideas or concerns out there. If your principal is not approachable, find a teacher or adviser who can advocate for you. The key is not to give up or get discouraged. Often change happens slowly, and in order for you to see it happen, you will need to be patient and persevere. What you learn in this process will not only help your school, but it will help develop skills you can use in the future. And the world will be a better place.

Am I passionate? Yes! It's how I was as a teacher. I went into administration because I believed it can be done as a whole school. Over the last five years, we've proved with staff and students that we can do it—we can create a school culture where every student is known well and learns well.

Epilogues. . .

From a Graduate

My name is Melanie Hornung, and I'm Teri—sort of. I match up with how she's focused on what's good for the school and wanting to learn more. I did make full use of the help periods, and I share the perspective that learning is fun. I have had great teachers that used my IEP to help me learn strategies and be an advocate for myself in my classes. And I did work in the office. That was a lot of fun and a great experience. One day Principal Steve Clarke walked through the front door and saw me sitting in the main office assistant's chair. He got a big smile on his face, said he was happy to see me and "it's about time we get someone in here who can take charge of the place." He made me laugh and feel important.

I can't really tell from the book what Teri is like outside of school though, like if she's interested in afterschool things. I really had school spirit and liked to participate in things like the Horseshoe Club.

I want everybody to know that Knownwell High School really can exist. Almost everything in it happened or could happen at my high school. During my freshman year, the House of Representatives was brand new. Clubs were getting formed for different things, and people were getting more involved with the school.

If there's a student or group of students that notice or talk about things at lunchtime, like they wish a department would be more academic or student friendly, they could talk to a counselor or one of the administrators. And their ideas would actually be acknowledged and would make a difference. The school would change from what they said. I can recognize counselors and teachers in the book. They're pretty familiar. It's not made up.

In fact, I'm pretty sure I know who Morris is. One of my classmates was named Austin. He would point out things that could be going better. He would talk to other students, and they would figure out a plan of what to do about it. Like pick a teacher on the staff who would be interested and would listen and start with that teacher.

My saddest part of high school was when I knew I would have to leave because of my dad's job in another state. I tried to take in as much as I could during my sophomore year, since I knew I was going to be moving. I cried. I talked to my counselor. When we said good-bye to Mr. Clarke— just the way he really does stand at the door every day—he said, "She can't leave. She's such a great kid." He went on describing how he liked having me there, and said I kept everybody on their toes in the office. My mom saw I was in tears, and I gave Mr. Clarke a big hug and he said, "You're always welcome back at BHS."

I was so homesick at my other school that I downloaded a picture of Bellingham High from the Web site and used it as my screen saver on my computer. I really got a contrast of how other high schools are *not* Known-well. The building was very old and needed to be painted. The equipment was old, and materials were in bad condition. What made it sad was that nobody seemed to care about fixing it up.

At BHS, students treat each other with respect and don't tease or make fun of people or spread nasty rumors. At the other school, they would start talking to me and I'd respond in a polite, interested way. And then they'd say, "Oh, that's not true. We're just pickin' with ya." Students didn't relate to each other seriously at all.

That was just the total opposite of Bellingham High. One thing that stands out so much is that the Collective Commitments really are the focus. It makes BHS so worth the time of being there and putting forth extra effort to learn. It's at least once a week or more that someone looks at or talks about the Collective Commitments—somebody realizes that's what the school is all about and that they should keep it that way. They get talked out of things they would do when they realize that's what the school is all about.

My entire freshman year I felt happier and more open at school than I even did at home. It was the way students treated other students and the way teachers treated everyone. There was respect all around.

The teachers in the other place I went were very "old school." I think they were back in the days of the 1970s and 1980s. Some teachers gave good grades just to students they liked, whether they earned them or not. There were some good teachers—but they were only teaching kids for the state test. They didn't really care about anything else or if you had interests you wanted to learn about.

My happiest time was when I found out we could move back to Bellingham for my senior year. I even went out and got senior pictures taken in that other state so they would get to BHS for the yearbook. That's what I love about Bellingham High. They just drew me back in as if I had never left. Besides my official senior picture, I got in the yearbook three times. There's one picture for participating in our class competition to "duct tape a student." It was only my second day back, and a friend of mine asked me if I would like to be taped to the wall. That made me feel like I meant something to the school. I was the senior getting duct taped. And in the end, the seniors won. And there's a picture that's captioned "Least likely to ever leave Bellingham"—because I just couldn't stay away. And there's a picture of me at senior prom, which was on my birthday.

If some people read this book and want to make their high school more like Knownwell High School, one thing they will have to do is be sure they have a principal with the potential. Like the principal in my other school was just a control freak. Nobody would be able to change him. But probably most principals could start by getting involved in events kids care about, like Homecoming games. Be more cheerful—that makes everybody happy. Have all the administrators and secretaries be more open and out there with the students monitoring, talking to students, talking to teachers. Be more open and willing to share ideas from any source, even students who aren't the popular ones or the straight-A types. Then you could really get somewhere to make school a better place.

And teachers could start out by watching what they say and how they act in front of kids. A famous phrase comes to my head: "If you don't have anything nice to say, don't say anything at all." Teachers should spread positive things about the school instead of pointing out all the errors or flaws.

They could start making their school more like Knownwell High School by meeting with a few students once or twice a week for two or three weeks. Just get their voices, their opinion, and their ideas of what they think about the school. Ask them if they would do one thing to make the school a better place, what would they do and how would they go about doing it? And then pick out a couple of more kids and get to know them. It doesn't have to be a big deal. Just make relationships a few at a time.

And students should step up and take some initiative too. If they want things different in their school, they shouldn't just wait for the adults to figure it out. First talk with the group they hang out with. Then talk with some upperclassmen. See what they can do to get other kids/students involved. Maybe even talk to a counselor or think of just one adult who they know will listen to their ideas. That's a place to start. Once they have talked 15–20 students into getting involved, set up a plan to get together at a certain place and time—maybe after school. Post it in the Commons so more kids could come and form a bigger group. There's really no excuse for not making the effort.

In conclusion, the most wonderful thing about my days at Bellingham High was Mr. Clarke standing at the door waiting for us in the morning and seeing us off at the end of the day. Most of the parents are off at work when the kids come and go. Knowing Mr. Clarke would be there was like having a parent who loved and cared for each student. Even teenagers need that.

Epilogues. . .

From a Student Leader

My name is Scott Frost—and I'm sort of Joe, but more of Morris. I'm like Joe because I'm an officially elected student leader—vice president of the student body. And I'm like Joe because I want to include more kids and I can see that even student organizations get stuck in ruts so I want to get ideas from more kinds of kids and make changes. The reason I'm more like Morris is that I'm involved with the whole school planning process and I'm working closely with Mr. Kupka, just like Morris worked closely with Mr. Spark.

This all got started when I was a sophomore and was wondering about some kids that just didn't seem to get with the program at Tremper High School. I really wanted more involvement of students in government and politics. So we set a goal in student government to try to get every student involved in at least one activity. And that goes along with the goal of the whole school that's on our newsletter and everything: Student Learning No Matter What.

We knew that learning doesn't only have to happen in the classroom—it can happen outside the classroom. So through talking with the student body president, we decided we could take this up as a student government goal and have an Activities Fair as a student government project. We figured that student *involvement,* no matter what, would really help move toward student *learning,* no matter what.

Over the summer, I worked to contact all the advisers of clubs and activities. At the start of school, the day before when the teachers were meeting, I announced to everyone to get advisers to sign on. It wasn't a piece of cake, by any means. There were a few teachers who didn't think it was necessary to have an Activities Fair, because they said the list of clubs is in the handbook and we don't need to take them out of class to find out about them. I responded as politely as I could—just talking to them. If you want teachers to be patient with kids, I had to be patient with them. I asked them what percentage of students they think would read every page in the handbook. They had to agree. The Activities Fair is a way for kids to see things and have some help readily available to sign up right there, instead of the longer process in the handbook. I told them it would show a wide range of possibilities. I even said that they might come to school more if they had a club they liked. So I got that across to the less willing teachers.

I worked with the teacher who had done the Activities Fair before without any student help or displays. We planned where each adviser's sign-up space would be. Then on September 9 we held the Activities Fair during second hour. Students came during each period—one wing at a time. They were only out of class about 20 to 30 minutes max. Each student came in and could explore 47 booths from sports and clubs and activities. There were displays of things those groups had done—and pictures and newsletters. There were activities I didn't even know were at Tremper. If I didn't know, how were other students going to know what's here for them? They would just think of the main sports and stuff and think nothing would fit them. It was really cool. You could see everybody going around to find out about these groups. Teachers said it was a success and that they were happy to see it. I knew a lot of teachers, but in this case I was getting other teachers coming up to me. It really felt good.

I would say that 75 percent to 80 percent of the students are signed up for something going on at Tremper. Hopefully, this will become an annual event—run by students for students. I know we got more freshmen to sign up for student government than we've ever had. And a school needs lots of leaders.

Of those who didn't sign up, I guess they just have a different agenda. They think school is just for formal education and you do other activities outside. They don't see what's available here. They're not getting the full education they could get, just the academic part. There's more that you can learn being in an activity about yourself and your strengths and how to work with others to make things happen. That's learning you need in real life, and you might use that more than the classroom learning, really.

In all of the work on this project, I was really impressed at the willingness of other teachers and students to become involved with learning and growing at Tremper. Through activities, you can become not just a number, but you can relate to the school. You can be a part and have a close connection to a coach or adviser and a bunch of kids throughout your whole four years. You can be more important to the school than just a student.

This is a big school. Everybody knows we're crowded, and there's going to be a referendum for a third comprehensive high school so we can be smaller in the future. But I like the way we can have a range of things—47 choices is a lot of opportunities at this time of life. You want to see all different aspects. When you get outside high school, there are all different kinds of people around you, and you need to have learned to relate in all kinds of situations. High school is a time for learning and being able to see what's there.

This project and my work with student government is what led me to sign on to the site planning team. Mr. Kupka came to me and asked me if I had any suggestions about changes for the high school, so I gave him some ideas. Then we talked in his office and he explained the site planning process to me and gave me some information to look at. I was excited to be one of the student members on the team, because I know that where Tremper High School goes is important to me. I don't want to just see some plans on paper, but be part of it. I want to know where plans and changes came from. I realized that I was being given a great opportunity—that I could have input and represent students with my own ideas but also those of other students who usually aren't heard.

But the first time I really understood was when I got there for the first two days of planning and the consultant explained how it would play out in the next two years. At the beginning, I was really curious to know how such a mixed group of almost 30 teachers and administrators and students and parents would ever come to a consensus. So many different people, ideas, and personalities. I honestly didn't think it would happen. Yes, I had some doubts. But the consultant kept assuring us it had happened before. So I had faith.

Before I got there, I didn't have any idea about whether I should hold back my ideas or just lay it all out there and say what I really thought and also what some other kinds of kids think. I looked around at the group and thought maybe I should hold back a little bit. But after about 30 minutes, I started believing I should give my opinions or I'd be passing up a chance to speak for my peers.

At first, it was a bit like going out on a limb. There were times when we were focusing on how all the problems are coming from the students. I said it's not always the students; it's the whole faculty and students combined that have to own up to problems and work to solve them.

I'd guess that probably 40 percent of all students would open up like I did and give their honest opinions. A lot of students feel that teachers have the final say and already know what they want. But some students have met the teachers and have been on teams and know they *will* listen. It's too bad that a greater percentage just come and don't really talk to their teachers. They'll say things to other students, but they're afraid of the teachers. It's not so much that teachers shut them down. It's more that they were taught to be respectful and they think that means adults don't want their opinions brought up. So they go along with the flow and choose to be followers instead of leaders. They don't see that coming along as a leader is much more important. I guess they haven't had the experience with a teacher-and-student bond yet.

The 60 percent would try to get things better for them and for those others that just come and don't engage. They might say to not have so much homework, that things should be easier. At least 40 percent want to maximize their chances. They want to be challenged and want experience to grow. Sometimes I hear all the students groaning and saying they don't have time and stuff. I think, What do you have to do that's more important? Everybody needs to get the most out of high school by combining the social part and the academic part.

Now there are a lot of changes going on at Tremper High School, and even more will be coming. The site planning team set objectives and chose the areas that we will work on, and I'm continuing on with one of the action teams. Our school was stuck, and now we're reinventing ourselves. We were going along all the same while everything else was changing— like the way it says "global society" in our mission. I'd say we're updating rather than totally changing. We don't need drastic change. We just need to reconsider the way we go about doing things and why and who they are benefiting. I can sense that there's a different vibe going through the school. It's just something you can sense.

Like in student government right now, we're updating the constitution, making things more current. We look at what's happening in the school. Some things are going up—like more discipline problems—and it seems like people are not motivated. Some things are down—less involvement, fewer bonds between students and staff. We were in more of a "come to school, get homework, go home do it, and bring it back" rut. There wasn't much interaction and no extra attention when kids needed it.

Now, through the whole Activities Fair and site planning, teachers are going out of their way to be more available and more present around students. Students will see teachers there for them and see how willing THS is to help them. Right now, if they're struggling learners, they're afraid. They need to see the teacher coming to them to ask what they need. But of course we don't want teachers helping them too much. They do need to get to the independence stage.

If I could, I would tell principals that it's not that hard to get student involvement. It just needs to be made public, and you need to say right out that you want to hear from students. If you show that students are important to you and believe our opinions are valid and show sincerity, you will get the students' response. If it's just "OK, thanks for your opinion," they won't respond as dramatically. Have one-on-one conversations, informally, with students rather than big general events. Having a history, developing a connection between you and a student, will really help. It can be on a small scale. Start with more of a previous relationship and tell individual students you know that you personally want their input. It will go through the grapevine, and then more students will start wanting to talk to you.

As far as teachers listening to students, the biggest problem is that they really never know where the student has come from and their history. Teachers should know that each student has his or her unique capabilities, and if you really try to find out their capacity, you'll appreciate your class much more. Then you'll have a stronger student and teacher bond, and that will really help. If you want more interaction, then work along with the principal. The principal can help mold the whole faculty as one, and there will be a big impact as one, not a separate, group.

And students need to try a little harder too. They should know that teachers have gone through the same things in life and high school as they have. Instead of keeping it in, teachers should bring that out and open the door. And students—don't be afraid of what the response from adults might be. When your principals and teachers give the chance and ask for your thoughts, take advantage of the chance. There was a little hesitation for me, but I realized I can't just hide my ideas inside and wish things would happen in my school. Nothing is going to happen unless you voice your opinion.

Epilogues. . .

From a Future Teacher

My name is Kacie Holcomb, and although I'm not in the book, I certainly would like to be. I didn't attend a school like Knownwell High, but I want to be a teacher in one. For as long as I can remember, I always wanted to have a job that seemed really important. I always felt like I needed to make a difference in many people's lives. In elementary school, I was determined to become the first female president. In junior high, I thought I wanted to be an emergency room physician. Today, I am proud to say that I'm going to college to become a high school social studies teacher and hopefully someday an administrator. I have always believed that getting a quality education is important for everyone, and good educators make it possible. Somewhere along the path to graduation, I realized I needed to be a part of that. Hopefully, I will be fortunate enough to do it at a place like Knownwell High School.

In May of 2005, I received my high school diploma with 27 other kids, the average graduating class size at my school. I started my education and graduated in the same K–12 facility in the small rural town I grew up in. Although the faculty did the best they could with what they had, I felt limited in course options and the extracurricular activities that were available. I believe that I would have been more prepared for college had I gone to a larger school. I have college classmates of the same ability level as me who are able to perform just as well in class without as much effort and who can take more advanced courses because they've had the preparation to do so. I had many positive educational experiences in high school, but I would argue that small schools are not necessarily the answer to getting a better education or building quality relationships. Instead, I believe all schools can be improved when the dedicated, outstanding individuals that can be found in them get involved.

As people work for better high schools, I believe the first thing to emphasize is the importance of communication between individuals—individuals like Mr. Spark and Morris. When individuals who generate ideas and inspiration communicate and collaborate to work as one force, great things can be accomplished. It is important to remember that a portion of these individuals are students. My peers and I could have made numerous contributions to help make our school a better place, but we were never asked.

As a student in a small school, I did feel "known well"—almost too well, because there was no privacy between personal and school life. I was constantly being compared to my older sister. Not to mention the numerous times I was actually addressed by her name, since all my teachers had her as a student too! But my ideas weren't known well. There wasn't any way to give input or express my opinions about school decisions.

Someday, I really do want to be a teacher in a school like Morris's. I want to be surrounded by coworkers, students, parents, and community members who care—people who want to and are willing to make a difference. I hope that I'll work for a principal who believes that the little things count, someone who realizes the impact that one individual can make. I hope that he or she helps make the school not only an excellent place for learning classroom material but also a place that provides positive opportunities for growth and development in all aspects of students' lives. I want to work with a principal who encourages students to believe they matter.

I want to be part of a group of teachers who set goals and strive to achieve them. I hope they encourage hard work and collaboration for the betterment of the school as a whole. I want to work with individuals willing to implement new practices and experiment with new approaches. I want to join others who are passionate about changing schools to change kids' lives.

In my classroom, I want to inspire my students to be excited about learning and making a difference. I want to be a positive role model like Mr. Spark is for the students at Knownwell High School. I hope to motivate students in an effort to help them find their own reasons for doing their best. And most of all, I want to listen to students and be sure that they have the necessary and important opportunities to be authentic stakeholders too.

Epilogues. . .

From the Author

My name is Edie Holcomb. I'm the author—and I'm a believer. I believe that high schools can be like Knownwell High School. I chose the name Knownwell High School because I believe any school can be "a humane, caring, and personalized school—a place where all students [are] welcomed, [are] *known well,* and [are] heard and, consequently, a place where all students [feel] a stake in the institution, not simply in their own success." I believe that "students learn to think best, to use their minds well, to try out ideas, to express their views, to interact in teams, and to absorb themselves in a dynamic learning process in an environment where they feel trusted, respected, and encouraged" (Mackin, as cited in NAASP, 1996, p. 11). I believe with Ted Sizer (NASSP, 2004, p. xi) that we serve students well by "taking a 'core mission' and playing it out in teaching and assessment in ways that reflect each student's strengths and weaknesses, learning styles and special needs . . . [and this] requires that each student be *known well.*"

I also chose the name Knownwell High School because every incident and every character represents true places and people that *I* have *known well.* I'm a believer because all the parts from the United States and Canada that make up this composite school are for real.

And the results are real. The student achievement data increases documented in Figure 22.2 *are authentic gains* made by Bellingham High School on the Washington State assessment. The impact of school culture on the marginal student and the special education student is real. Teri and Mike and Gloria represent true cases I've observed up close and personal.

I believe in leaders like Mr. Spark and Mr. Clarke and many others who are my heroes. If you think the story sounds too perfect or too easy, go back and read between the lines and you will see the human resistance and the logistical barriers. I didn't focus on them, because this kind of leader doesn't focus on them. Principals who increase student engagement and student achievement do it by unceasing, unwavering intention and attention to the culture around them. They convey a vision and reinforce a shared mission. They hold themselves and their schools accountable by reviewing their results—celebrating and frequently repeating evidence of progress to stimulate the energy and hope to keep adjusting and improving. They listen and modify deadlines and timelines in response to human frailty, without ever taking their eyes off the goal. They set parameters, rather than dictate details. They engage everyone to whom it matters, and they make sure everyone knows who matters most: the students.

The Winter Olympics have just concluded. Some teams slammed the puck and each other up and down the ice. Some teams set a stone in motion and carefully and quietly swept a path to glide it to its target. I believe in change leaders who have the intensity of hockey and the patience and finesse of curling.

"The idea for comprehensive change may not begin in the principal's office, but it most assuredly can end there either through incomplete planning, failure to involve others, neglect, or failure to create conditions that allow a new order of things to emerge in the high school. Creating those conditions is often the first challenge—and sometimes it must start within the principal's own thinking and interaction with people" (NASSP, 2004, p. 20). I believe in thoughtful leaders who look first at themselves and model more than mandate the changes they want to see.

I believe in teachers. In the most difficult school I've known, there were stars to hitch the wagon to. In the most highly regarded schools, there were trolls under the bridge to the future. Under the toughest skins, I have often found hearts that have been hurt and fires that have been dampened—but can be rekindled. The voices of students who want to learn and participate fully in their schools can get under those skins.

And I believe in students. From the knee-hugging kindergarteners to the eye-rolling, shoulder-shrugging teenagers, I believe they want to do well and they want to make things better. I could make a long list of the Morrises (and Dorises) I've met in schools—some actively engaged, some waiting on the periphery to be invited to the dance. They see, perhaps more clearly than we, what needs to be addressed. I believe in the Lupitos and Gabriellas and the Takeshas and Shaquilles—who want us to know them well too.

As I send this off to the reviewers and the editors and the production staff, I feel like Mr. Spark at graduation. It's hard to say good-bye to Morris and Joe and Mike and Tom and Teri and Gloria and send them on to you. I want to say to you, "Listen to them, they are wise. Don't squelch them, they are our hope." I want to say to them, "Go for it! In your quiet ways, you rocked your school. Go out and rock your world."

I have a feeling they will be *known well.*

References

Allen, R. (2004, August). Making high schools better: Reform groups search for answers far and near. *Education Update*, pp. 4–6.

Allen, R. (2005, November). Personal learning plans link present to future. *Education Update*, pp. 4–5, 8.

Argyris, C., & Schön, D. A. (1974). *Theory in practice: Increasing professional effectiveness.* San Francisco: Jossey-Bass.

Association for Supervision and Curriculum Development. (n.d.). *Differentiating instruction.* Retrieved January 24, 2004, from www.ascd.org/trainingopportu nities/pdonline.html.

Barell, J. (1995). *Critical issue: Working toward student self-direction and personal efficacy as educational goals.* North Central Regional Educational Laboratory. Retrieved February 24, 2006, from www.ncrd.org/sdrs/areas/issues.

Bloom, B. S. (Ed.). (1956). *Taxonomy of educational objectives: The classification of educational goals, Book 1: Cognitive domain.* New York: Longmans.

Blum, R. W. (2005). A case for school connectedness. *Educational Leadership, 62*(7): 16–20.

Blythe, T., Allen, D., & Powell, B. S. (1999). *Looking together at student work: A companion guide to assessing student learning.* New York: Teachers College Press.

Boys' academic slide calls for accelerated attention. (2003, December 22). *USA Today.* Retrieved December 29, 2003, from www.usatoday.com/usatonline/20031222/5779049.shtm.

Burmaster, E. (2004). *Wisconsin toolkit for service-learning and citizenship.* Madison: Wisconsin Department of Public Instruction.

Calgary Board of Education. (2005, May 6). *Alternative High School—Calgary, Alberta, Canada.* Retrieved May 12, 2005, from http://lschools.cbe.ab.ca/b863.

Corbett, D., Wilson, B., & Williams, B. (2005). No choice but success. *Educational Leadership, 62*(6): 8–12.

Covey, S. (2004). *The eighth habit: From effectiveness to greatness.* New York: Free Press.

Cushman, K. (2005). Subjects or citizens? High school students talk about investing in their schools. *Phi Delta Kappan, 87*(4): 316–319, 323.

Downey, C., Steffy, B. E., English, F. W., Fraser, L. E., & Poston, W. K. (2004). *The three-minute classroom walk-through: Changing school supervisory practice one teacher at a time.* Thousand Oaks, CA: Corwin Press.

Easton, L. (2002, April 10). Lessons from learners: For this alternative school, listening to students is the best reform strategy. *Education Week,* pp. 33–35.

Easton, L. (Ed.). (2004). *Powerful designs for professional learning* (pp. 43–52). Oxford, OH: National Staff Development Council.

Fletcher, A. (2003). *Meaningful Student Involvement: Guide to Inclusive School Change.* Retrieved from www.soundout.org.

Franklin, J. (2005). Removing the emotional roadblocks in education. *Education Update, 47*(11): 1–3, 8.

Gewertz, C. (2006, January 18). Philadelphia: Students advocate changes in test procedures. *Education Week,* pp. 5–12.

Goodwin, B. (2000). *Policy brief: Raising the achievement of low-performing students.* Aurora, CO: Mid-Continent Research for Education and Learning.

Grier, P. (2000, April 20). Journey into the land of cargo pants. *Christian Science Monitor.* Retrieved November 3, 2004, from csmonitor.com/cgibin/durable Redirect.pl?/durable/2000/04/20/fpls2-csm.shtml.

Grindeland, S. (2005, December 25). Ordinary people, extraordinary gifts. *The Seattle Times,* p. A16.

Gurian, M. (2002). *Boys and girls learn differently.* Hoboken, NJ: John Wiley & Sons.

Heath, D. (2000, March 15). Psychological bars to school improvement. *Education Week.* Retrieved June 19, 2000, from www.edweek.org/ew/ew_printstory .cfm?slug=27heath.h19.

Holcomb, E. L. (1991). *School-based instructional leadership: Staff development for teacher and school effectiveness.* Madison, WI: National Center for Effective Schools.

Holcomb, E. L. (2001). *Asking the right questions: Techniques for collaboration and school change* (2nd ed.). Thousand Oaks, CA: Corwin Press.

Holcomb, E. L. (2004). *Getting excited about data: Combining people, passion, and proof to maximize student achievement.* Thousand Oaks, CA: Corwin Press.

Hunter, R. (2004). *Madeline Hunter's mastery teaching: Increasing instructional effectiveness in elementary and secondary schools* (updated ed.). Thousand Oaks, CA: Corwin Press.

Johnson, R. S. (2002). *Using data to close the achievement gap: How to measure equity in our schools.* Thousand Oaks, CA: Corwin Press.

Klem, A. M., & Connell, J. P. (2004). Relationships matter: Linking teacher support to student engagement and achievement. *Journal of School Health 74*(7): 262–273.

Lambert, M. B. (Ed.). (2003, May). Student involvement. *The Learning Network,* pp. 1–3.

Lampert, J. (2005). Easing the transition to high school. *Educational Leadership (62)*7: 61–63.

MacLaury, S. (2002) *Student advisories in Grades 5–12: A facilitator's guide.* Norwood, MA: Christopher-Gordon.

Marzano, R. J. (2003). *What works in schools: Translating research into action.* Alexandria, VA: Association for Supervision and Curriculum Development.

Marzano, R. J. (with Marzano, J. S., & Pickering, D. J.). (2003). *Classroom management that works: Research-based strategies for every teacher.* Alexandria, VA: Association for Supervision and Curriculum Development.

Marzano, R. J., Pickering, D. J., & Pollock, J. E. (2001). *Classroom instruction that works: Research-based strategies for increasing student achievement.* Alexandria, VA: Association for Supervision and Curriculum Development.

McCauley, M. B. (2005, May 24). Matching boys with books. *Christian Science Monitor.* Retrieved June 2, 2005, from www.csmonitor.com/2005/0524/p11s01-legn.html.

McLaughlin, M. W. (1994). Somebody knows my name. In *Issues in Restructuring Schools* (Issue Report No. 7, pp. 9–12). Madison, WI: University of Wisconsin-Madison, School of Education, Center on Organization and Restructuring of Schools. (ERIC Document Reproduction Service No. ED 376 565)

Mundy, A. (2005, February 27). Gates "appalled" by high schools. *Seattle Times.* Retrieved February 1, 2006, from seattletimes.nwsource.com/html/localnews/2002191433_gates27m.html.

Murphy, J., Beck, L. G., Crawford, M. W., Hodges, A., & McGaughy, C. L. (2001). *The productive high school: Creating personalized academic communities.* Thousand Oaks, CA: Corwin Press.

National Association of Secondary School Principals. (1996). *Breaking ranks: Changing an American institution.* Reston, VA: Author.

National Association of Secondary School Principals. (2004). *Breaking ranks II: Strategies for leading high school reform.* Reston, VA: Author.

National Staff Development Council. (2006, February). What a school leader needs to know about walk-throughs. *The Learning Principal,* pp. 4–5.

Osofsky, D., Sinner, G., & Wolk, D. (2003). *Changing systems to personalize learning: The power of advisories.* Providence, RI: Education Alliance at Brown University.

Platt, A. D., Tripp, C. E., Ogden, W. R., & Fraser, R. G. (2000). *The skillful leader: Confronting mediocre teaching.* Acton, MA: Ready About Press.

Pope, D. C., & Simon, R. (2005). Help for stressed students. *Educational Leadership, 62*(7): 33–37.

Richardson, J. (2004, November). Leading the way: Houston teachers play key roles in school improvement initiative. *Results,* pp. 1, 6–7.

Rothstein, A. (2006, February 8). Students as coaches: One high school's experiment in using student's perceptions to help teacher improve instruction. *Education Week,* pp. 31–32.

Roy, P. (2006). A new role: Cultural architect. *The Learning Principal, 1*(4): 3.

Schmoker, M. (2004, October). High school as it could be: From cacophony to continuous improvement. *SEDL Letter,* pp. 3–7.

Senge, P. (1990). *The fifth discipline: The art and practice of the learning organization.* New York: Doubleday.

Serrano, A. (2005, March 3). Striving to succeed. *The Honolulu Advertiser,* pp. E1, E5.

Shannon, G. S., & Bylsma, P. (2003). *Nine characteristics of high-performing schools.* Olympia, WA: Office of Superintendent of Public Instruction.

Sizer, N. (n.d.). Shaping school culture. *Resources for small schools.* Retrieved February 23, 2005, from http://ali.apple/com/ali_sites/ali/exhibits/1000488.

Sizer, T. (1992). *Horace's school: Redesigning the American high school.* Boston: Houghton Mifflin.

Sousa, D. (1999). *Brain-based learning: The video program for how the brain learns.* Thousand Oaks, CA: Corwin Press.

Sousa, D. (2001). *How the special needs brain learns.* Thousand Oaks, CA: Corwin Press.

Sousa, D. (2002a). *How the gifted brain learns.* Thousand Oaks, CA: Corwin Press.

Sousa, D. (2002b). *How the special needs brain learns* (Video). Thousand Oaks, CA: Corwin Press.

Sousa, D. (2003). *The leadership brain: How to lead today's schools more effectively.* Thousand Oaks, CA: Corwin Press.

Sousa, D. (2005). *How the brain learns* (3rd ed.). Thousand Oaks, CA: Corwin Press.

Sousa, D. (2006a). *Facilitator's guide to How the Brain Learns* (3rd ed.). Thousand Oaks, CA: Corwin Press.

Sousa, D. (2006b). *How the brain learns: The four-book collection.* Thousand Oaks, CA: Corwin Press.

Sousa, D., Nielsen, L. B., Zionts, P. N., Thurlow, M. L., & Bender, W. N. (2003). *2004 special education teacher induction kit.* Thousand Oaks, CA: Corwin Press.

Sparks, D. (2006). Practice the discipline of committed listening. *The Learning Principal, 1*(4): 2.

Spence, C. (2005). *Creating a literacy environment for boys.* Toronto, Canada: Thomson Nelson.

Sroka, S. (2006). Listening to the whole child. *Education Update, 48*(1), 1, 8.

Stover, D. (2005, December). Climate and culture: Why your board should pay attention to the attitudes of students and staff. *American School Board Journal,* pp. 30–32.

Studer, S. (2001, Spring). Restorative justice at Boulder High School: A student's perspective. *Restorative Justice in Action Newsletter.* Retrieved March 3, 2006, from www.coloradorestorativejustice.org/publications/schools2001.pdf.

Tovani, C. (2000). *I read it, but I don't get it: Comprehension strategies for adolescent readers.* Portland, ME: Stenhouse.

Tovani, C. (2004). *Do I really have to teach reading: Content comprehension, Grades 6–12.* Portland, ME: Stenhouse.

Vaughan, A. (2005). The self-paced student. *Educational Leadership, 62*(7): 69–73.

Washington State Office of Superintendent of Public Instruction. (2004a). *Mathematics: K–10 grade level expectations.* Olympia, WA: Author.

Washington State Office of Superintendent of Public Instruction. (2004b). *Navigation 101: How a focus on planning skills leads to higher student performance.* Olympia, WA: Author.

Wehlage, G. G., Rutter, R. A., Smith, G. A., & Lesko, N. (1989). *Reducing the risks: Schools as communities of support.* New York: Falmer.

What Kids Can Do. (n.d.). *In their own words: Student perspectives.* Retrieved February 26, 2006, from www.whatkidscando.org.

Wilce, H. (2006, February 16). The school where pupils rate their teachers. *The Independent.* Retrieved March 10, 2006, from http://education.independent.co.uk/schools/article345645.ece.

Wilson, B. L., & Corcoran, T. B. (1988). *Successful secondary schools: Visions of excellence in American public education.* New York: Falmer.

Index

CORWIN PRESS

The Corwin Press logo—a raven striding across an open book—represents the union of courage and learning. Corwin Press is committed to improving education for all learners by publishing books and other professional development resources for those serving the field of PreK–12 education. By providing practical, hands-on materials, Corwin Press continues to carry out the promise of its motto: **"Helping Educators Do Their Work Better."**

NATIONAL ASSOCIATION OF SECONDARY SCHOOL PRINCIPALS